W9-BBS-119

WITHDRAWN

WITHDRAWN

TWENTIETH CENTURY
INTERPRETATIONS
OF
INVISIBLE MAN

PS
3555
.L625
I537

TWENTIETH CENTURY INTERPRETATIONS
OF
INVISIBLE MAN

A Collection of Critical Essays

Edited by
JOHN M. REILLY

Prentice-Hall, Inc. *Englewood Cliffs, N. J.*
A SPECTRUM BOOK

SALEM COLLEGE LIBRARY
WINSTON-SALEM, N. C.

Quotations from *Invisible Man* used by permission of Random House, Inc. Copyright 1947, 1952 by Ralph Ellison.

Copyright © 1970 by Prentice-Hall, Inc., Englewood Cliffs, New Jersey. A SPEC-TRUM BOOK. All rights reserved. No part of this book may be reproduced in any form or by any means without permission in writing from the publisher. C–13-505495-8; P–13-505487-7. *Library of Congress Catalog Card Number 70–126822.* Printed in the United States of America.

Current printing (last number):
10 9 8 7 6 5 4 3 2 1

PRENTICE-HALL INTERNATIONAL, INC. (*London*)
PRENTICE-HALL OF AUSTRALIA, PTY. LTD. (*Sydney*)
PRENTICE-HALL OF CANADA, LTD. (*Toronto*)
PRENTICE-HALL OF INDIA PRIVATE LIMITED (*New Delhi*)
PRENTICE-HALL OF JAPAN, INC. (*Tokyo*)

Contents

v   85578

Introduction

by John M. Reilly

As if he were the positive counterpart of his fictional character Rine-hart, Ralph Ellison characteristically speaks of his life in America as reflecting a variety of styles. Recounting his youth in Oklahoma, he describes himself and his friends as aspiring to the completeness of Renaissance men; writing of his musical education, he points out that he not only learned the popular Southwest jazz but also received a solid classical training in public school and later at Tuskegee Institute. Ellison does not misrepresent himself. An outline of his biography shows, in fact, the rich variety that is the basis of his self-conception.

Born March 1, 1914, in Oklahoma City, to where his parents had recently moved from South Carolina, Ellison's eventual concern with individual identity in a democratic society was anticipated in his father's gesture of naming him Ralph Waldo in honor of Emerson. When Ralph was a young child, his father died, leaving him to be reared in the way of many black youngsters of his time and place—working at a variety of part-time jobs and moving freely about the streets and shoeshine parlors, and, of course, receiving his formal education in the racially segregated schools. Certainly school and other institutions made him aware of the restrictions placed upon him by the accident of his color, but since Oklahoma was considerably less rigid about caste than the older South, he learned quite early that the black life style as observed among musicians, for example, included ways of transcending those restrictions.

In his youth he was deeply impressed by black cultural heroes in jazz as well as in folk life. It was they who helped to nurture the image of Renaissance man in Ellison's imagination, for unlike the pusil-lanimous "Toms," the musicians and folk heroes appeared to act with-out compromise. The last phrase must be reiterated—without compromise. For though he speaks optimistically at times about American life, Ellison is not an accommodationist who adjusts himself willingly to caste restrictions. The feeling of satisfaction with his life that he projects derives from a sense of cultural completeness, affirming life's quality in a black culture.

Because Ellison did well in school in Oklahoma city, he earned a state scholarship, which he used to attend Tuskegee Institute. There, from 1933 to 1936, he studied music with William L. Dawson, the classical conductor and composer, then went north to take up sculpture under Richmond Barthé. Arrival in Harlem further broadened his contacts with black culture. Very soon he met Richard Wright, who had himself recently arrived in Harlem, and Langston Hughes, a vigorous spokesman of popular black culture, who had come to Harlem in the 1920s, when it was the capital city for the "New Negro." In this way, Ellison became attached to a chain of relationships running from the artists who made a "Harlem Renaissance," still vigorously alive in the work of Hughes, to Wright, who would father the major Afro-American fiction of the 1940s.

In 1936, Richard Wright was known to the small audience of left-wing literary magazines as a poet, though Ellison soon found him to be an ambitious, self-disciplined author of fiction too. The stimulation of Wright, perhaps to a degree his example also, brought Ellison to develop yet a third talent—writing. His first published piece was a review in *New Challenge,* a journal edited by Wright, who also encouraged his subsequent attempts at fiction. Like most artists in the 1930s, whether aspiring or established, Ellison had to work at a variety of tasks. He was, for example, briefly a counterman at a YMCA, and briefly a clerk-receptionist for the psychiatrist Harry Stack Sullivan. He even spent part of one year with his brother near Dayton, Ohio, where they supported themselves by hunting game. The most important event of this period was, however, his settling in New York, for that brought about his involvement in the most significant movement in Afro-American history after the abolition of slavery—the Great Migration. Though his parents too had known an early phase of that migration out of the older South, he himself had the great good fortune—consequent, no doubt, upon desire—to find through Wright, Hughes, and the residue of the New Negro movement a conscious artistic concern with the meaning of the black diaspora.

In the 1920s black artists had celebrated the folk culture transplanted to the cities, and had stressed the positive values of being black. The economic and social experience of the thirties altered celebration to protest against the general racism that had stifled the blacks' hope of gaining freedom through simple migration from the old South. Hence, by the time Ellison got to Harlem he found his fellow artists examining the relation of their work to left-wing politics, seeking the connection between protest and revolution. Inevitably, like Wright and Himes and others, he served a literary apprenticeship to radicalism, and throughout the thirties used for his primary literary outlet *The New Masses,* where he published a number of sketches, short stories, reviews, and feature reports. Though stimulated by this experience to attend carefully to social conflict and cause, he seems not to have made a deep emotional commitment to revolution. His eventual anti-communism shows little ferocity of one who has been betrayed.

With his apprenticeship complete, Ellison began the application of his energies to deliberate thought and writing that resulted in his masterpiece. Some of his earlier work—those stories in *The New Masses*, for example—contain the seeds of the later novel in their representation of the innocence of young black boys transformed by knowledge of death, sex, and race; yet it was not till the wartime years when Ellison was nearing thirty years of age, that the varied experiences of his life focused in the creation of a major narrative. From that point his biography, for students of literature, is the record of the gestation of *Invisible Man*.

His attempt to enlist in the U.S. Navy band having been rejected, Ellison served a time in the Merchant Marine, then returned from sea and service in 1945 to a farm in Vermont, where he began to work on his novel in earnest. In interviews he has said that he first intended to write a novel about a Negro flyer. The short story "Flying Home" (1944), an earlier use of the subject, tells of a black pilot who crashes into an Alabama cotton field and finds in a lengthy dialogue with a black peasant that he remains rooted in folk life despite his aspirations to rise above it. As he thought further about his novel, however, Ellison became concerned with the idea of Negro leadership, even studying Lord Raglan's *The Hero* for its insights; but soon, again according to his own statement in interviews, the idea of a Negro hero led him to an antiheroic conception of Negro invisibility. A portion of the novel—the Battle Royal section of chapter 1—was at length published in 1947 (in *Horizon* in England and later in the American magazine *'48*), but the completed book did not appear for another four years. Its story had by that time become the story of Ellison's discovery of the meaning of his experience as an individual and as an Afro-American. Each choice of incident and each decision about technique had been tailored to communicate simultaneously a sense of the protagonist's character and personality and a sense of the typically black aspects of his experience.

The National Book Award given to *Invisible Man* in 1953, drew attention to Ellison's status as a major contemporary author. Among black authors, participation in innumerable panels and forums on the "Negro problem" has usually been a function of popularity, but in Ellison's case the experience has so far been different and more complimentary. The literary and journalistic establishment has not thought him to be a Negro spokesman so much as an author successful *despite his being Negro,* and in that way a contrast to sensational black protest writers.

The academic establishment has also shown interest in Ellison. His academic appointments have included an instructorship of American literature at Bard College, the Alexander White Visiting Professorship at the University of Chicago (1961), a professorship of creative writing at Rutgers (1962–64), and a continuing appointment as Fellow in American Studies at Yale (1964).

The initial reception of *Invisible Man* among reviewers writing for a general audience was largely favorable. Dissent came in statements written by black authors in politically left publications. The theme of black identity attracted most approval, though nearly every reviewer was dissatisfied with what seemed to be inconsistencies in the structure of the novel. Much of the reviewers' praise took the form of noting that Ellison had written a "universal" book. In the words of one reviewer, for example, *"Invisible Man* is not a great Negro novel; it is a work of art any contemporary writer could point to with pride."* [1]

Its date of publication serves as the best clue to reviewers' indifference about the novel's "blackness." *Invisible Man* was published two years before the Supreme Court decision in *Brown* v. *Board of Education* struck down school segregation, eight years before the sit-in movement began at North Carolina A & T College, to say nothing of the succeeding political and black nationalist movements. Moreover, the 1950s were a time when intellectuals and writers—always excepting those politically on the left and the most sensitive of the black critics—seemed to prefer books that featured introspection in search of the tragic universal presumed to exist in human nature to accounts of social or cultural conflict. Protest fiction was widely held to be outmoded, and ethnic or political consciousness was condemned for producing sterotypical instead of typical representations of reality. To many of Ellison's white contemporaries *Invisible Man* seemed simply a book of the times. It represented for them the work of a Negro intellectual trying to create an identity that would transcend social differences, that would in effect "integrate" the Negro intellectual into the experience that white intellectuals liked to call the "mainstream."

Since the 1950s *Invisible Man* has continued to have a favorable audience and is now one of the established classics of post-war fiction, widely read by informed people and widely studied in formal literature classes. Too often, however, discussion of the book continues from the premise that *Invisible Man* is a book about a universal

[1] Harvey Curtis Webster, "Inside a Dark Shell," *Saturday Review,* XXXV (April 12, 1952), 22–23.

identity crisis, told by means of a black protagonist,[2] a premise that at this point in time considerably misrepresents it. For the fact is that Ellison's novel is very definitely an Afro-American book. His way of writing in it decidedly illuminates and expresses Afro-American culture. Mary Rambo and Peter Wheatstraw, Lucius Brockway and Rinehart and Ras—all of these characters, secondary in the novel, come from the primary reality—black life. And so do the narrative style of Trueblood, the speech of the vets of the Golden Day, and Bledsoe's rationalizations.

The novel is not, however, simply a slice of popular black life. It has at its core a concept of Afro-America that was given classical expression by W. E. B. DuBois in *The Souls of Black Folk*. America, DuBois wrote, has allowed the black man to see himself only through the revelation of others.

> It is a peculiar sensation, this double-consciousness, this sense of always looking at one's self through the eyes of others, of measuring one's soul by the tape of a world that looks on in amused contempt and pity. One ever feels his twoness,—an American, a Negro; two souls, two thoughts, two unreconciled strivings; two warring ideals in one dark body, whose dogged strength alone keeps it from being torn asunder.[3]

DuBois's statement describes a consciousness of ambiguity that in turn derives from social circumstances. Allowing as much as we may for individual difference and variety, a common experience and some common reactions are nevertheless certain to be shared among any group who share the same social circumstances. This shared consciousness was DuBois's subject, and it has become, almost inevitably, the crucial subject of most Afro-American authors in the twentieth century. Ellison's particular vehicle of that consciousness in *Invisible Man* is his unnamed first-person narrator.

An instructive contrast can be made between Ellison's representation of consciousness by the first-person point of view and previous black writing. Wright's *Native Son* and Ann Petry's *The Street*, for example, are both third-person narrations in which the author tries nevertheless to reveal the inner consciousness of the protagonist

[2] For a discussion of the novel from the rather different point of view that it is not committed enough to black protest, consult the controversial exchange between Ellison and Irving Howe. Howe's essay "Black Boys and Native Sons" appearing in *Dissent* (Autumn 1963) argued that Baldwin and Ellison had fallen away from the tradition of protest established by Richard Wright. Ellison replied to Howe, Howe responded, and finally Ellison concluded the discussion, all in the *New Leader* early in 1964. Howe's portion of the debate is reprinted in *A World More Attractive* (New York: Horizon Press, 1963), pp. 98–122, and excerpted in part 2 of the present volume (see pp. 101–2). Ellison has reprinted his side under the title "The World and the Jug" in *Shadow and Act* (New York: Random House, 1964), pp. 107–43.

[3] In the essay "Of Our Spiritual Strivings," *The Souls of Black Folk: Essays and Sketches* (Chicago, 1903). Quoted from Fawcett Premier edition, pp. 16–17.

by authorial description of feelings. Wright may have chosen third-person narration because his protagonist was largely inarticulate. Petry's reasoning must have been different, but in both cases the authors keep an authorial presence in their novels to describe environment directly.

Ellison, in contrast to Wright or Petry, advances character consciousness to the center of the narrative and assumes rather than describes the role of social circumstances in developing consciousness. I believe it is this difference of technique that leads some people to misread *Invisible Man*. Because of the first-person story told by an articulate narrator searching for his personal identity, many readers have felt that Ellison demotes protest. But this is decidedly not the case. The Battle Royal in the opening chapter, or the speech of Homer Barbee in the fifth, the experience at the Liberty Paint plant, the riot, and so on, are all scenes through which Ellison reaches back of his narrator's consciousness to attack the social circumstances that oppress black people in America.

From the time of Frederick Douglass's autobiographies, black authors have observed the connection between personal troubles—the subject of the blues—and the general collective experience giving rise to them. They cannot write about private feelings without remembering social context. And *Invisible Man* is no exception to this Afro-American manner. At one and the same time it explores the theme of personal identity and reveals the conditions in the environment that make the narrator's troubles. The first theme works out in the foreground of the narrator's consciousness, the second in the experiences he records and their symbolic revelations.

Stylistically considered, *Invisible Man* shares with the modernist writings of, say, Eliot or Faulkner—to name two nonblack authors of whom Ellison is fond—an attempt to represent the ambiguity of subjectively perceived experience. This is not because Ellison treats another type of reality than Wright or Petry, one more removed from the barricades, but because he conceives of social reality differently. Generally, the esthetics of realism requires that a writer describe what he sees in an unadulterated way, since realist esthetics emphasizes clarity of perception and freedom from illusion. The revolution in modern esthetics, however, has tended to shift attention from perception to *conception*. Modernist writers have been exceptionally aware of the influences exercised upon the artist's way of conceiving reality by his acceptance of one or other ideology, and the consequence has been to lay stress upon the fact that reality has multiple faces. So it is with *Invisible Man*. A novel titled and fashioned overtly to direct attention to the process of perception is actually charged by an idea *about* perception. Ellison denies our usual processes of sight on the one hand, while trying on the other to give us new sight.

The metaphor of his title points to our ways of seeing literature as well as to our ways of seeing black people written about in literature.

The epilogue and prologue are the keys to the structure and the meaning of *Invisible Man*. Speaking in the prologue, the narrator establishes that all he is about to relate has already happened, in the objective sense, and therefore exists now in his consciousness. The distinction between exterior reality and interior sensibility is thus erased. Moreover, in the vision induced by jazz and pot he enters into a spatial scene through the temporality of music and makes clear that time and space are also merged in his consciousness. Like any opening scene in fiction or establishing shot in cinema, the prologue constitutes a contract between author and reader. Ellison is saying to the reader that his viewpoint is surreal, and the reader must accede to his style of vision or misunderstand what follows in the more conventional narrative.

If we accept the contract presented in his prologue, then the outrages of the Battle Royal symbolism, the uncertainty about sanity in the Golden Day, the machine rebirth, and all the other ironies of the book are enriched. Realism and symbolism come together, united in the narrator's mind, the locus of complex meanings. His mind and, therefore, his narrative contain the ambiguities, the multiple responses to caste, that we are expected to understand exist simultaneously. Then the epilogue of the novel, coming after the nightmare of the Harlem riot and together with the narrator's sense of greater control over his destiny, returns us to the terms of the contract, reminding us that the reality of *Invisible Man* must be dealt with at the level of mind.

"In going underground," the narrator says, "I whipped it all except the mind, the *mind*." He goes on to say that "the mind that has conceived a plan of living must never lose sight of the chaos against which that pattern was conceived." The esthetics of the novel has become the philosophy of the narrator.

There is one further step. The narrator will probably have to surface, "since," he says, "there's a possibility that even an invisible man has a socially responsible role to play." So the unnamed narrator, now free of the definitions others imposed upon him, is about to become engaged in the world on his own terms, with his own viewpoint. But we remember that this has not been a novel of his gradual arrival at that viewpoint. He has had it all along; the prologue made that clear. His knowledge that there are multiple conceptions of reality has informed his entire story and hovered above each moment of choice.

The narrator's various attitudes toward white society—from early accommodations to eventual repudiation—have counterparts in the collective history of Afro-America as well as in the personal lives of the citizens of the black nation; yet, as the narrator relates his experience, these stages have both a past and present significance. He has already lived his moments of choice, but their anguish has made his present consciousness. Equivocal? Indeed it is. Ellison's unnamed narrator, poised at the moment of a totally free commitment to the world, brings one period in Afro-American literary history to fulfillment. The absurdity, ambiguity, and irrationality of caste experience that so many authors have documented coalesces in an existentially self-aware figure who serves as archetype of the black experience in America.

Ever since the success of *Invisible Man*, Ellison reportedly has been at work on another novel. After nearly two decades, the second novel has yet to appear. The fiction he has published—"And Hickman Arrives" (*Noble Savage*, 1960) and "It Always Breaks Out" (*Partisan Review*, Spring 1963)—is rich with the feel of black life rendered surrealistically as in *Invisible Man*. Still, Ellison is in danger of remaining one of those American phenomena that foreign critics are fond of observing—a one-book author. He remains an active critic of literature and a fine essayist but has not transformed his insights into full-length narrative. Each of the pieces named above is episodic.

Perhaps Ellison put so much of the experience he knows into *Invisible Man* that he cannot write another novel without fear of repeating himself; or perhaps, as his narrator puts it, he has not yet whipped it in his mind and cannot come out of his symbolic hibernation with a new fictional identity that relates to the rapidly changing contemporary struggle for black liberation. But such speculation by a critic is presumptuous. It is more pertinent to note the curious relationship between Ellison and a new generation of black writers that his silence and his example provoke.

In 1965, *Book Week* conducted a poll of predominantly white critics and found them saying that the most distinguished novel of the previous two decades had been *Invisible Man*. Three years later another poll, this one conducted by *Negro Digest* (now known as *Black World*), offered an interesting modification of *Book Week*'s findings. The editors of *Negro Digest* surveyed young black authors, asking about their attitudes toward predecessors and requesting statements about their relationship to the emerging Black Esthetic. Some of the young authors cited *Invisible Man* as a most important novel, but they were by no means in the majority. Moreover, they did not speak of Ellison as an author to be emulated, and there were even some who thought him today irrelevant. Final evaluation of Ellison's influence, however, will have to take account of a subtler matter. The surreal vision that so impresses one in *Invisible Man* and that prodded some critics to find it a departure from Afro-American literary practice is actually a vision frequently shared by younger black writers, including some in the *Negro*

Digest poll. Influence may be the wrong term to describe the relationship between *Invisible Man,* Himes' *Pinktoes* (1961), Jones' short *Tales* (1967), Charles Wright's *The Wig* (1967), and Ishmael Reed's *The Free-Lance Pallbearers* (1967), but the fact remains that all of these writers adopt a surreal vision of reality and represent current black-white relationships as absurd, upended. Whether Ellison provided the example or anticipated a trend, his work, stylistically considered, offers a conception of experience that is appropriate, and has been widely appropriated by his successors, to description of the feeling of being black in America. If indeed we do learn to see by learning to read our conceptual maps, then *Invisible Man* will remain one of the best guides we have to a uniquely American reality.

Leadership Mirages as Antagonists in *Invisible Man*

by M. K. Singleton

The affirmations of Ralph Waldo Ellison's powerful first novel, *Invisible Man*, echo, as Earl Rovit has intimated (*Wisconsin Studies*, Fall 1960),[1] the values of Ellison's name-sake, Ralph Waldo Emerson. The novel, in fusing bookishly derivative metaphor and down-to-earth observation, also draws upon the influence of such diverse spirits as Thomas Wolfe, T. S. Eliot, Booker T. Washington, and James Joyce. Although rhetorical problems arise from Ellison's eclectic style, and although some of the novel's scenes are better rendered than others of the scenes, Ellison's chronologically straightforward narrative technique resolves adequately, and at times remarkably, the formal problems basic to his story. Critics have not explained, however, the thematic strand made up of elusive, yet penetrating, references to Negro leadership, references which develop into a full-scale transcendentalist critique of the more stereotyped and stagnant forms of twentieth-century Negro leadership. The lights and cross-lights which Ellison throws on this aspect of the Negro experience are not easily identifiable as such: the leadership motifs are more often evoked than spelled out, and the clue to an entire ideology is sometimes little more than a salutation ("Peace, it's wonderful"), an epithet ("Uncle Tom"), or a name ("Marcus Garvey," "Frederick Douglass," etc.).

The Negro leader most often mentioned in the text of *Invisible Man* is Booker T. Washington. The unnamed hero of Ellison's narrative is, during his pre-invisibility stages of growth, essentially a public speaker, and it is as a public speaker that he becomes implicated in the idiom of Booker T. Washington. Oratory, whether on street corner, in pulpit,

---

"Leadership Mirages as Antagonists in Invisible Man*" by M. K. Singleton. From* Arizona Quarterly, *XXII (Summer 1966), 157–71. Copyright © 1966 by* Arizona Quarterly. *Reprinted by permission of* Arizona Quarterly.

[1] [See this volume, pp. 56–63—Ed.]

SALEM COLLEGE LIBRARY

WINSTON-SALEM, N. C.

or on rostrum, remains a vital part of Negro culture; and the hero's progress from nonage to philosophical independence is mirrored in his public utterances. The hero accurately identifies himself in the novel's Prologue as "an orator, a rabble rouser," and, although by the close of the novel his voice, as a function of his partial alienation, has become "disembodied," he has achieved an idiom of his own. From his first "public address" as a tot in an Easter program (he forgot the words) through his high school graduation speech, his college declamations, his extemporaneous anti-eviction harangue, his Brotherhood addresses, his funeral oration for Tod Clifton, the hero develops an individualism antipathetic to the manipulative and the reductive. This growth of sensibility is communicated by Ellison through bird imagery which so pervades *Invisible Man* as to make it a true *parlement* of fowls; and the most insistent of these bird images is of the mockingbird, whose songs are popularly known to derive from those of other birds, but whose medley, as naturalists know, features a melody of its very own.

With this oratorical context in mind, the fact that the hero's high school and college years witness dreams of becoming "a potential Booker T. Washington" should not be surprising, since Washington was not only the best-known Negro leader before Martin Luther King, but was also a talented speaker. Ellison was more than ordinarily exposed to the ideology of Washington because of Ellison's attendance for several years at Tuskegee Institute, which Washington founded in 1881 to save the Negro from degradation by training him in Christian virtue, farming, and the mechanical arts, and patience. Ellison's grasp of Washington's great transitional services to the Negro people is matched only by his recognition that Washington's vista of hope could sag into fatuity. Students of Negro leadership ideology have had no difficulty in discovering what Ellison dramatizes as "the black rite of Horatio Alger" latent in Washington's writings ("Every persecuted individual and race should get much consolation out of the great human law which is universal and eternal, that merit, no matter under what skin found, is in the long run, recognized and rewarded"). Examples of Ellison's usage of Washington's figurative language are particularly evident in the opening chapters of the novel. The hero feels pathos in the fact that the freed Negroes were told "that they were free, united with others of our country in everything social, separate like the fingers of the hand. And they believed it." This passage, echoing the language of Washington's address at the Atlanta Exposition of 1895, prepares for the speech the narrator gives after the Battle Royal before an assemblage of Caucasian city fathers whose inattention and disrespect in itself goes far to undercut the Washington theory of merit-and-sure-reward. In his graduation speech the lad slavishly elaborates the "Cast down your bucket where you are" metaphor made famous in Washington's *Up From Slavery*, and an arc of tension is defined between the two fragments of Washington's rhetoric by the youth's inadvertent lapse into the phrase "Social . . . equality," a lapse which draws upon him the ire of the audience and the need to recant. The narrator momentarily forgot Washington's policy of accommodating the whites' social prejudice (Washington accompanied his "separate as the fingers of the hand" trope with the following unmistakable admonition: "The wisest among my race understand that the agitation of questions of social equality is the extremist folly"). Washington's outward social conservatism was for the sake of securing from the whites financial support for his schools; and, indeed, the youth himself is abjectly dependent on the white leaders for a scholarship. But again, it should be stressed that Ellison is not primarily interested in discrediting a leadership ideology which had great provisional merit and which provided simplistic directives enabling generations of Negros to achieve a measure of dignity.

Ellison's major fictional strategy is, rather, to chronicle his hero's picaresque misadventures at the hands of assorted exponents of some distorted variant of Washington's credo. The first half of *Invisible Man* is a *tour de force* sequence which sees the narrator, before his faith is finally shaken, take more pratfalls on behalf of the Horatio Alger dream than any fictional character since Lemuel Pitkin, the anti-hero of Nathanael West's *A Cool Million.*

The narrator's first deep insight into conventional power and its possibilities occurs during his attendance at the Tuskegee-like college. The college president, Dr. Bledsoe, fills with outward plausibility the outlines of the dedicated Booker T. Washington type of leader. His picture in the Negro newspapers is impressively captioned "EDUCATOR," and the narrator, though not impressed that Bledsoe owned "not one, but *two* Cadillacs," felt a certain awe toward him: "He was our leader and our magic. . . . He was our coal-black daddy of whom we were afraid." The narrator learns grounds for fear of Bledsoe when the student mismanaged a chauffering duty and caused distress to a wealthy white benefactor of the college. Not only does Bledsoe expel the morally blameless student, but he does so in a cruel manner, maliciously concealing the finality of the hero's expulsion and otherwise hurting his prospects. From his visits to the president's office to receive his disciplining, however, the student gains insight into raw power and its warping effects. Bledsoe's character is patterned in part after that of Charles Dickens' Uriah Heep: by acting humble, Bledsoe rose from the post of college swineherd to the college presidency; and this succession to the presidency is hardly less ritualized than the apostolic succession itself. To support the impression that he incarnates the Founder's values, Bledsoe arranges for Negro guest preachers who will eulogize him, and one such preacher fervently insinuates that Bledsoe incarnates the Founder as well as the Founder's values. The narrator admits to total belief in the Founder's scheme of salvation, weighted as that scheme is in white, middle-class objectives: "I would . . . teach others to rise up as he wished them to, teach them to be thrifty, decent, upright citizens, contributing to the welfare of all, shunning all but the straight and narrow path." But even the youthful protégé could feel an oppressive quality to the Founder's bosky panorama of docile mechanics and artisans. On the campus stood a bronze statue of the Founder, "his hands outstretched in the breathtaking gesture of lifting a veil that flutters in hard, metallic folds above the face of a kneeling slave," yet the narrator confesses puzzlement as to "whether the veil is really being lifted, or lowered more firmly in place." In the narrator's cryptic blasphemy lurks more even than the Emersonian judgment that institutions ideally are merely the ground on which Man Individuated might project himself.

On one occasion when Bledsoe shapes his face into the lineaments of fawning solicitude for Mr. Norton, the narrator sees above the scene a portrait of the Founder looking remotely down at him, "benign, sad, and in that hot instant, profoundly disillusioned. Then a veil seemed to fall." When next the veil was lifted, in Bledsoe's office, the disciplined student was made privy to the smug force rankling beneath the Washingtonian veneer: "Power doesn't have to show off. Power is confident, self-assuring, self-starting and self-stopping, self-warming and self-justifying. . . . This is a power set-up, son, and I'm at the controls." Bledsoe then relates his dicta on power to his personal career: "It's a nasty deal and I don't always like it myself. . . . But I've made my place in it and I'll have every Negro in the country hanging on tree limbs by morning if it means staying where I am. . . . I had to be strong and purposeful to get where I am. I had to wait and plan and lick around." When the president next interviews the hero, before sending him away on a rigged-job quest northward, the bland Washingtonian mask of "up-lift" is recomposed: "Two things our people must do is accept responsibility for their acts and avoid becoming bitter. . . . Son, if you don't become bitter, nothing can stop you from success." Unfortunately the veil also had returned to its place, and the hero fails to fathom the old knave's malice.

Even were Bledsoe less an opportunist in seeking to exploit the Founder's vision, the vision's stultifyingly mechanical nature becomes apparent. The hero grows depressed when looking at the fading snapshots of the anonymous Negroes living in the bleak Reconstruction era: the snapshots of an opaque and sodden people showed them, grouped around their mule-drawn wagons, more caged in allegory than liberated by any expansive promises inherent in the American Dream. Indeed, their foreshortened and insistently racial "history" tended to keep them insulated from full emancipation.

In opposition to the racial tableaux was one of the hero's college literature professors, who, in lecturing on Joyce's *A Portrait of the Artist as a Young Man,* asserted that "Stephen's problem, like ours, was not actually one of creating the uncreated conscience of his race, but of creating the *uncreated features of his face.* Our task is that of making ourselves individuals." Combined with this literary subversion is the subversion evidenced by the narrator's grandfather's flash of irreducible humanity as he lay on his death-bed. Still, on the campus, the druidic chapel speakers see to it that the wicker cages in which the contemporary Negro students are immolated ("minds laced up, eyes blind like those of robots") are artfully woven and rewoven.

The feasibility of Booker T. Washington's simple plan is further eroded by the secondary characters in *Invisible Man.* One critic of Washington's values, the "mad vet," is one of a band of World War I veterans committed to an asylum. Many of these Negroes had worked their way into the professions before their confinement, and thus their waggeries at the expense of the college are informed with a certain sad wisdom. The "mad vet," who had been trained as a surgeon, was relegated to the asylum as an aftermath to his having crossed the color line to perform an operation on a white woman. The "mad vet" dubs the narrator a "mechanical man" for his supposed willingness to be an "automaton . . . a thing and not a man . . . amorphous." The ex-surgeon's accusations jibe with Norton's identification of the student-narrator as a cog in an educational machine whose output enables the benefactor gloatingly to quantify: the school marches out "three hundred teachers, seven hundred trained mechanics, eight hundred skilled farmers, and so on." And the narrator, from first to last, is threatened and afflicted by an assortment of machines, although he comes to cry out against these anti-transcendental "things." He gradually assumes the romantically defiant stance of the legendary John Henry.

The anti-machine theme, as related to the skepticism regarding Booker T. Washington's plan for Negro improvement, crests in the paint factory scene. Brockway represents unqualified success in the Washington mode: his mastery of the paint mixing operation makes him indispensable to a large, otherwise modern, factory. He boasts, "we are the machines inside the machine," and his white employer is compelled to respect his unique grasp of paint-base cookery. Nevertheless, the youthful narrator can in part take the measure of this subterranean Merlin. Brockway, however successful outwardly, is even more insecure than Bledsoe. He is beset on the one side by unionized workers who decry him as an "Uncle Tom" (to which Brockway replies: " 'Here the white man done give 'em jobs,' he wheezed as though pleading a case. 'He done give 'em *good* jobs too, and they so ungrateful they goes and joins up with that backbiting union!' "). On the other side the old man fears educated engineers, whom he sees as trying to edge him out of his job. But the narrator is unable, although he aspires to become a leader of his people, to bring to terms even the insecure Brockway. The would-be leader is too prone to fantasies and posturing: "Bledsoe . . . was never out of our minds. That was a secret of leadership"; "It always helped at the college to be a little different, especially of you wished to play a leading role," etc. Such coxcombical reflections about the need of strut and prominence are Ellison's clue that the narrator is, midway through the story, merely a green, unripened leader.

In Jim Trueblood's story the anti-machine, anti-Horatio Alger, anti-conventional themes flow together, and Ellison's Trueblood theme is kept before the reader by a succession of pawky, unreconstructed Trueblood gargoyles (as Peter Wheatstraw). Trueblood's robust personal philosophy undercuts several of the novel's rascals, especially Norton, the philanthropist. Trueblood, at the extreme bottom of the social heap, and roundly despised by the Negroes associated with college "up-lift," makes top-heavy—if not absurd—Bledsoe's espousal of the Booker T. Washington assertion that "possession of property is an evidence of mental discipline, mental grasp, and control. It is also evidence of self-sacrifice, economy, industry, fixedness of character, and purpose." Although abjectly poor, Trueblood emerges from *Invisible Man* as one of the few undeniably authentic heroes of sensibility in modern literature. His family problem is juxtaposed to Norton's own so-called "first-hand organizing of human life," and Trueblood's candor, perception, singing ability, and power as storyteller blend into a worthy style, a style likened by the narrator (and, implicitly, by Trueblood himself) to a "manly" daddy quail. Norton's style, of which his ill-motivated philanthropy is a figment, is altogether infected by shabby evasion: his sublimation of his incestuous desire into a grandiose but nonetheless platitudinous educational plan has small claim to admiration. Such "style" as Norton pretends to wobbles between the fatuous Ivy League idiom ("I know my life rather well") to the language of boiler-plate charity ("I also construct a living memorial to my daughter"). Ellison intends for the reader to compare Norton's limp pessimism, as revealed in Norton's paraphrase of Thoreau ("the human stock goes on, even though it degenerates") with Trueblood's fatherly pride in his daughter's appearance: "You know, we gettin' to be a better-lookin' race of people."

That the poor farmer's adventure becomes a prime perspective from which specious values are later satirized must be emphasized, since more than one hasty reader has, after a careless analysis of the values underlying the Trueblood saga, found bewildering the remainder of *Invisible Man*. Likewise, to be distracted by Trueblood's explanation of the heterosexual event is to risk missing the irony in the share-cropper's apparent acceptance, by having formulated his story as a quasi-confessional, of blame for the act. The author sets out ample detail for the reader to see Trueblood's lapse as sociologically determined; thus Trueblood's foxy and gratuitous moral speculations, during his compromised awakening, add up to an incisive spoof of the ancient tradition of didactic meddling by casuists in intimacy. Indeed, Trueblood's verbal admission of blameworthiness is merely a token offering to the authoritarian gods of respectability unsurpassed in audacity since Jim and Huck Finn gave up persimmon theft.

Nor, conversely, should the outward respectability of Norton be allowed to camouflage his emotional make-up. His prurient compulsion to hear the sharecropper's tale is fed by his need to define and redefine his own "whiteness": not simply his shoes, but his entire being, could be described as "white, trimmed with black." Norton's psychic life is luridly glorified, in his own eyes, by the reductive use of supposedly animalistic Negroes as "trim." (The narrator comes to understand this easy paradox in the paint factory scene, whereby adding drops of inky black acid to yellow-white paint and stirring, he transmutes the paint into a dazzling white.) In developing this fictional critique, Ellison shows his agreement with John Stuart Mill's belief that, "of all the vulgar modes of escaping from the consideration of the effect of social and moral influences upon the human mind, the most vulgar is that of attributing the diversities of conduct and character to inherent natural differences." This insight is so important that the Golden Day episode is used to establish that animality is part of the human condition, and the narrator draws the reader's attention to such details as Norton's "animal-like teeth," while Edna states the folklore endocrinology of "rich ole white men." These clues that even the altruistic Norton may have a certain ingrown carnality throw into question his philosophy of "up-lift" by defining his lack of self-knowledge. Equally important to the thematic unfolding of the novel is the problem caused by the infliction upon the Negro of the stereotype of blithe sensuality: it is in sober recognition of the force and prevalence of these stereotypes that Ellison feels he must universalize, and make humorous, the sex drive of the Caucasian.

The clichés about the emotional make-up of the Negro received encouragement from Alain Locke's theory of a uniquely vitalistic Negro sensibility; and the survival of the clichés, not only among Caucasian jazz fans, but even among Negroes themselves, has created a perennial snag for Negro leadership. In *Invisible Man* we see distorted versions of the theories of Alain Locke—and some analogous ideas which pre-date Locke's writings—trouble not only the Booker T. Washington program, but every other redemptive vision as well.

During the 1920's, when a fashionable white novelist could without a second thought entitle a novel about Harlem *Nigger Heaven,* Alain Locke found support, especially among sophisticated Caucasians, for his advocacy of the Negro in America as potentially a soulful, artistic elite. In 1928, Locke praised the Negro temperament for "its hedonism, its nonchalance, its spontaneity," and he stated that "the reaction against over-sophistication has opened our eyes to the values of the primitive and the importance for the man of emotions and untarnished instinct." Therefore, concluded the essayist, "the revolt against conventionality, against Puritanism, has found a strong ally in the half-submerged paganism of the Negro." Although Locke ceaselessly strove to update and modify these ideas, it is also true, as dramatized in *Invisible Man,* that versions of the Lockean *mystique* could be twisted by self-serving whites, since the idea that Negroes might somehow embody a soulful primitivism and power would easily elide back into myths about the Negro which had currency long before the decade of Locke, Sherwood Anderson, and Eugene O'Neill.

Whatever the cultural source of the Negro stereotypes in *Invisible Man,* when the narrator is himself pressed into one of the molds, his reaction typically is muffled humor. When one white woman attempts to vamp him, announcing that the hero's voice is "*primitive*; no one has told you, Brother, that at times you have tom-toms beating in your voice?" he slyly identifies the rhythm as the beat "of profound ideas." When another white woman wishes to be buffeted by a savage, the hero jests: "What's happening here . . . a new birth of a nation?"; and when a third white woman deplores his mere ginger-shading, he laments: "maybe she wants to see me sweat coal tar, ink, shoe polish, graphite, what was I, a man or a natural resource?" When, however, other Negro characters are made to yield to one of the reductive molds, the narrator's resilient humor abandons him. There can be nothing amusing in the thought that even the manly Trueblood can be weakened and undone by dreaming about Mr. Broadnax's morally enervating saying about "niggahs." Again and again in the novel, what appears to the white outsider as zesty hedonism is more truly fatalism.

Tod Clifton's apostasy features a more deliberate, and thus more troubling, acquiescence in a Negro stereotype. Clifton is defined as an outstanding political activist, but so deep is his disillusionment with the Brotherhood movement that he not only abandons his leadership role, but he also takes to huckstering on street corners. His wares are grinning orange-and-black tissue paper dolls which dance when strings are twitched, and his spiel includes bitter jibes at the political opiate he is hawking:

> *Shake him, shake him, you cannot break him*
> *For he's Sambo, the dancing, Sambo, the prancing,*
> *Sambo the entrancing, Sambo Boogie Woogie paper doll.*
> *And all for twenty-five cents, the quarter part of a dollar . . .*
>   *. . . he'll kill your depression*

*And your dispossession, he lives upon the sunshine of your
lordly smile. . . .*

To fully plumb the narrator's shock at Clifton's willingness to swap
activism for the nadir of commercialism, the reader must recollect the
hero's distaste for other versions of the dancing doll. For instance, when
the hero was solicited by the young Calamus Club member to be the
"Jim" on his well-appointed raft, the hero's attention significantly
focusses on a shoeshine boy across the street dancing for pennies. And
when later the narrator writhed in shock therapy and an intern sees
his contortions as "dancing" ("They really do have rhythm, don't
they? Get hot, boy!"), he reacts with anger. Throughout the novel,
dancing is associated with hopelessness. Indeed, as he states of the
dancing doll, "The political equivalent of such entertainment is death."
As to Tod Clifton, the lost leader, this is precise; but the insight is
appropriate as well to other forms of leadership broached in the novel.

The narrator's emergence as a leader occurs during the eviction
scene. This scene not only defines the enormity of the leadership
vacuum, but it also brings alive historical realities which had remained
mute in the Reconstruction snapshots in the college "museum."
Among the belongings of the old folks, and those which most catch
the narrator's eye, are the ex-slave's "free papers," a small Ethiopian
flag, a tintype of Lincoln, a yellowing newspaper portrait of a black
man (captioned: MARCUS GARVEY DEPORTED), a tomato plant, and three
lapsed life insurance policies. With these and other concrete tokens
before him, the narrator can shape his hortative address into an
effective call to resistance. The textual sign that the hero is now fit to
respond when the mob calls for a leader is given in the "I yam what I
am!" passage: he is no longer compelled to "eat Northern" and is
thereby emancipated. His success in synthesizing history out of the
litter of meager belongings is also a personal victory: in finding what
Ike McCaslin found in the yellowed commissary ledgers in *The Bear*
and what Jack Burden found during his historical researches in *All the
King's Men,* the narrator enables himself finally to come to terms
with the dark, tangled underworld of the ancestral past.

The narrator, however, must mature beyond his conventional barricades, triumph before he can say anything very profound about the
nature of the leadership vacuum. Clifton accounted for the vacuum by
positing a soddenness, an inertia, on the part of the Harlem citizenry:
speaking of Garvey, Clifton paid the great Negro nationalist a tribute:
"He *must* have had something to move all these people! Our people
are *hell* to move." But the narrator is gradually made to see how all
leadership is provisional; and this theme is suggested by the repetition
of the name of Frederick Douglass, the nineteenth-century leader
who arose from the ranks of slavery to press for citizenship rights for

the Negro. The narrator comes to see even his eviction harangue as a function of the will of the assembled crowd and himself as "Perhaps an accident, like Douglass." And Douglass, the hero elsewhere tells us, in becoming an orator instead of a boatwright, had simply become himself and defined himself.

In the Harlem disturbance bringing the book to a close is shown an effective leadership rising out of the masses. Dupre, Scofield, and others lead themselves on missions defined by themselves, and, in view of their wit and skill, their thanks to the narrator for having "led" them is ironic. Ellison takes care, however, to set off against his affirmation of Representative Men in Harlem the scenes wherein his point-of-view narrator is threatened by strong-arm groups. Still, Ellison's essential optimism can best be seen by comparing his closing scenes with those of two other authors whose philosophies are more pessimistic. In both William Golding's *Lord of the Flies* and Mark Twain's *A Connecticut Yankee* the decent characters whose aspirations toward representative leadership are as legitimate as could be proposed in the given near-savage state of society are shown vulnerable to un-refined, reactionary usurpation. Ellison's vision of human possibility compels him to spare his point-of-view narrator from the spear of the outlandish knight. Ellison thus attempts to enlarge his definition of the human condition beyond the disillusion which continues to pervade Golding's works and which led the elderly Twain to despair, shortly before his death, that mankind will insist upon having its kings.

Other leadership strands are, of course, present in *Invisible Man*, and, although they add nothing different to the above thematic asser-tion, they variously support and deepen it. Ras the Exhorter builds a pan-African black nationalist group by embroidering on Harlem's memory of Garvey's West Indian-nurtured answers to the racial prob-lem, but Ras's downfall is as much destined by his reversionary credo as by his outlandish African costume. Equally implausible is the Brotherhood's Stalinist black-white collective leadership. The Brother-hood's abstract disregard for the realities of Harlem strongly encourages the narrator to think for himself; and his thoughts increasingly high-light the false-leader theme. He envisions as his and society's antagonist a universal leadership composite made up of leaders altruistic and cynical, Negro and Caucasian. The mirages emitted by Man Leading go far toward making absurd the idea of a Good Follower and go far toward accounting for Rinehart's practical nihilism. Rinehart, a protean demi-leader, very profitably caters to many of Harlem's follies. While Rinehart's lack of social responsibility is, of course, deplorable, Rinehart's concurrent styles usefully reveal to the narrator the liber-ating aspects of role-playing.

Instead of leadership from without, the hero's endorsement of his grandfather's supposed belief that the better course is "to affirm the principle on which the country was built" is explicitly juxtaposed to worship of particular leaders. Ellison's elaboration of this in the Epilogue becomes vividly Emersonian. The dislike of R. W. Emerson for the linear and his liking for the concentrically spherical, is mirrored in Ellison's anti-Euclidean description of his hero's starting point: the narrator is said to have "lived a public life and attempted to function under the assumption that the world was solid and all the relationships therein." But the hero's misadventures qualify him as seer. He warns that "the old eagle" will "rock dangerously" unless putative leaders hearken: "the mind that has conceived a plan of living must never lose sight of the chaos against which that pattern was conceived. That goes for societies as well as individuals." This blunt underpinning supports the point-of-view character's unmistakably Emersonian concluding grandiloquence: "Whence all this passion toward conformity anyway?—diversity is the word. Let man keep his many parts and you'll have no tyrant states. . . . America is woven of many strands; I would recognize them and let it so remain."

It could be argued that Ellison's leadership blues in *Invisible Man,* although relevant to the Negro dilemma through the 1940's, have become "dated" by the rise of such articulate leaders as Martin Luther King, James Baldwin, and Dick Gregory, and such energetic organizations as now abound. There are, however, two answers to this charge. First, the Watts affair illustrates the vitality of the leaderless strata, as well as the existence of such a class, nearly twenty years after the publication of *Invisible Man.* Second, and more important, no art form's theme *per se* "dates" it if the theme is at once concrete and universal. Even if Watts remains an anachronistic fluke, Ellison's novel, like Diogenes' tub, squarely rests "on its own bottom."

Ralph Ellison and the Uses of Imagination

by Robert Bone

. . . In 1933 Ellison enrolled at Tuskegee Institute to study composition under William Dawson, the Negro conductor and composer. In his sophomore year, however, he came upon a copy of *The Waste Land*, and the long transition from trumpet to typewriter had begun. He read widely in American fiction and, initially scorning the moderns, developed a lifelong devotion to the nineteenth-century masters. On coming to New York in 1936 he met Richard Wright, who introduced him on the one hand to the prefaces of Conrad and the letters of Dostoevski, and on the other to the orbit of the Communist party. One evening he accompanied Wright to a fund-raising affair for the Spanish Loyalists, where he met both Malraux and Leadbelly for the first time. It was a notable occasion, symbolic of the times and of the cross-pressures exerted from the first upon his art.

From these cross-pressures Ellison derived his most enduring themes. How could he interpret and extend, define and yet elaborate upon the folk culture of the American Negro and, at the same time, assimilate the most advanced techniques of modern literature? How could he affirm his dedication to the cause of Negro freedom without succumbing to the stridencies of protest fiction, without relinquishing his complex sense of life? In *Shadow and Act,* Ellison returns again and again to these tangled themes: the relationship of Negro folk culture to American culture as a whole, and the responsibility of the Negro artist to his ethnic group.

As instrumentalist and composer, Ellison had faced these issues for the better part of two decades. When he began to write, it was natural for him to draw upon his musical experience for guidelines and perspectives. Not that his approach to writing is merely an extension of an earlier approach to jazz and the blues; they tend, in fact, to rein-

From "Ralph Ellison and the Uses of Imagination" by Robert Bone. Copyright © 1966 by Robert Bone. Originally appeared in Anger and Beyond, *ed. Herbert Hill (New York: Harper & Row Publishers, 1966), pp. 86–111. Reprinted by permission of the author.*

Ellipses indicate omission of some biographical discussion and consideration of political and other influences.

force each other. But his experience with jazz was formative; it left a permanent mark upon his style. His controlling metaphors are musical, and if we are to grasp his thought, we must trace his language to its source. There, in the world of Louis Armstrong and Charlie Parker, Bessie Smith and Jimmy Rushing, we may discover the foundations of Ellison's aesthetic.

Music

The essence of jazz is group improvisation. Its most impressive effects are achieved, according to Ellison, when a delicate balance is maintained between the individual performer and the group. The form itself, consisting of a series of solo "breaks" within a framework of standard chord progressions, encourages this balance. "Each true jazz moment," Ellison explains, "springs from a contest in which each artist challenges all the rest; each solo flight, or improvisation, represents (like the successive canvases of a painter) a definition of his identity: as individual, as member of the collectivity, and as a link in the chain of tradition." "True jazz," he concludes, "is an art of individual assertion within and against the group."

Here is a working model for the Negro writer. By balancing conflicting claims upon his art, he can solve his deepest problems of divided loyalty. As an artist with a special function to perform within the Negro group, the writer must be careful to preserve his individuality. He must learn to operate "within and against the group," allowing neither claim to cancel out the other. Similarly on the cultural plane, where the Negro's group identity is at stake. Here the writer can affirm whatever is uniquely Negro in his background while insisting precisely on the American quality of his experience. "The point of our struggle," writes Ellison, "is to be both Negro and American and to bring about that condition in American society in which this would be possible."

Closely related to the question of individual and group identity is that of personal and traditional styles. Every jazz musician must strike a balance between tradition and experimentation, for "jazz finds its very life in an endless improvisation upon traditional materials." It follows that no jazzman is free to repudiate the past. The jam session, where he must display a knowledge of traditional techniques, will see to that. He must master "the intonations, the mute work, manipulation of timbre, the body of traditional styles" before he can presume to speak in his own voice. The path, in short, to self-expression lies through what is given, what has gone before.

As an American Negro writer, Ellison inherits a double obligation to the past. He must become familiar with a folk tradition which is his alone, and with a wider literary culture which he shares. Moreover, he must strive in both dimensions for a proper blend of past and present, given and improvised. In describing his response to his folk tradition, Ellison draws a parallel to the work of Picasso: "Why, he's the greatest wrestler with forms and techniques of them all. Just the same, he's never abandoned the old symbolic forms of Spanish art: the guitar, the bull, daggers, women, shawls, veils, mirrors." Similarly, Ellison appropriates folkloristic elements from Negro culture, embroiders on them, adapts them to his literary aims, and lifts them to the level of a conscious art.

In the wider context of American literature, the same principles apply. Consider Ellison's experimental idiom. Not since Jean Toomer has a Negro novelist been so inventive of new forms, new language, new technical devices. And yet none has been so deeply immersed in the American literary past. As Ellison struggles toward the realization of a personal style, he is *improvising* on the achievement of our nineteenth-century masters. It is this body of writing, he insists, "to which I was most attached and through which . . . I would find my own voice, and to which I was challenged, by way of achieving myself, to make some small contribution, and to whose composite picture of reality I was obligated to offer some necessary modifications."

Still a third balance must be struck between constraint and spontaneity, discipline and freedom. For the jazzman owes his freedom to the confident possession of technique. From his own struggles with the trumpet, Ellison learned how much the wild ecstatic moment depends on patient hours of practice and rehearsal. Freedom, he perceived, is never absolute, but rooted in its opposite. The game is not to cast off all restraint but to achieve, within the arbitrary limits of a musical tradition, a transcendent freedom. Jazz taught Ellison a respect for limits, even as it revealed the possibility of overcoming limits through technique. It was the blues, however, that taught him to discern in this paradox an emblem of the human condition.

The blues arise out of a tension between circumstance and possibility. The grim reality that gives them birth bespeaks the limits and restrictions, the barriers and thwartings, which the universe opposes to the human will. But the tough response that is the blues bespeaks a moral courage, a spiritual freedom, a sense of human possibility, which more than balances the scales. In Ellison's words, "The blues is an art of ambiguity, an assertion of the irrepressibly human over all circumstance whether created by others or by one's own human failings. They are the only consistent art in the United States which constantly reminds us of our limitations while encouraging us to see how far we can actually go."

The blues begin with personal disaster. They speak of flooded farmlands and blighted crops, of love betrayed and lovers parted, of the black man's poverty and the white man's justice. But what matters is the human response to these events. For the blues are a poetic confrontation of reality. They are a form of spiritual discipline, a means of transcending the painful conditions with which they deal. The crucial feature of the blues response is the margin of freedom it proclaims. To call them an art of ambiguity is to assert that no man is entirely the victim of circumstance. Within limits, there is always choice and will. Thinking of this inner freedom, Ellison speaks of "the secular existentialism of the blues."

This sense of possibility lies at the center of Ellison's art. It explains his devotion to his craft, for what is technique but another name for possibility? It explains his attitude toward protest fiction, for the propaganda novel, in portraying the Negro primarily as victim, gives more weight to circumstance than possibility. Ellison's is a more plastic sensibility. His heroes are not victims but adventurers. They journey toward the possible in all ignorance of accepted limits. In the course of their travels, they shed their illusions and come to terms with reality. They are, in short, picaresque heroes, full of "rash efforts, quixotic gestures, hopeful testings of the complexity of the known and the given."

If circumstance often enough elicits tears, possibility may release a saving laughter. This blend of emotion, mixed in some ancient cauldron of the human spirit, is characteristic of the blues. It is a lyricism better sampled than described. Note in Ellison's example how the painful humiliation of the bird is controlled, or absorbed, or even converted into triumph by a kind of grudging laughter:

> Oh they picked poor robin clean
> They picked poor robin clean
> They tied poor robin to a stump
> Lord, they picked all the feathers
> Round from robin's rump
> Oh they picked poor robin clean.

The blues have nothing to do with the consolations of philosophy. They are a means of neutralizing one emotion with another, in the same way that alkalies can neutralize an acid stomach. For the American Negro, they are a means of prophylaxis, a specific for the prevention of spiritual ulcers. It is not a question of laughing away one's troubles in any superficial sense, but of gazing steadily at pain while perceiving its comic aspect. Ellison regards this tragicomic sensibility as the most precious feature of his Negro heritage. From it stems his lyrical intensity and the complex interplay of tragic and comic elements which is the distinguishing mark of his fiction.

If the blues are primarily an expression of personal emotion, they also serve a group need. Perhaps the point can best be made through a comparison with gospel singing. When Mahalia Jackson sings in church, she performs a ritual function. Her music serves "to prepare the congregation for the minister's message, to make it receptive to the spirit and, with effects of voice and rhythm, to evoke a shared community of experience." Similarly in the secular context of the blues. When Jimmy Rushing presided over a Saturday night dance in Oklahoma City, he was acting as the leader of a public rite: "It was when Jimmy's voice began to soar with the spirit of the blues that the dancers—and the musicians—achieved that feeling of communion which was the true meaning of the public jazz dance."

We are dealing here with substitute rituals. During an epoch which has witnessed the widespread breakdown of traditional religious forms, Ellison finds in jazz and the blues, as Hemingway found in the bullfight, a code of conduct and a ceremonial framework for his art. "True novels," he insists, "arise out of an impulse to celebrate human life and therefore are ritualistic and ceremonial at their core." Ellison perceives, in short, the priestly office of the modern artist and assumes the role of celebrant in his own work. Like the blues singer, he is motivated by an impulse to restore to others a sense of the wholeness of their lives.

Finally, specific features of Ellison's literary style may be traced to his musical background. His fondness for paradox and ambiguity, for example, derives from the blues: "There is a mystery in the whiteness of blackness, the innocence of evil and the evil of innocence, though being initiates Negroes express the joke of it in the blues." The changing styles of *Invisible Man* (from naturalism to expressionism to surrealism, as Ellison describes the sequence) are based on the principle of modulation. Chord progressions in jazz are called "changes"; they correspond in speed and abruptness to Ellison's sense of American reality, the swift flow of sound and sudden changes of key suggesting the fluidity and discontinuity of American life.

Literature

Let us now turn from Ellison's musical to his literary heritage. We must begin with the picaresque novel and attempt to explain why this form, which first appeared in Renaissance Spain, should be revived by a contemporary Negro novelist. We must then consider Ellison's affinity for the American transcendentalists, in light of his commitment to the picaresque. Finally, we must examine in some detail two devices that are central to his art.

The picaresque novel emerged toward the end of the feudal and the beginning of the bourgeois epoch. Its characteristic hero, part rogue and part outlaw, transcended all established norms of conduct and violated all ideas of social hierarchy. For with the breakdown of static social relations, a testing of personal limits, a bold confrontation with the new and untried became necessary. Hence the picaresque journey, no longer a religious quest or pilgrimage but a journey toward experience, adventure, personal freedom. It was the journey of the bourgeois soul toward possibility, toward a freedom possessed by neither serf nor lord under the old regime.

It can hardly be an accident that *Invisible Man* and *The Adventures of Augie March* should win the National Fiction Award within two years of one another. Nor that Ellison and Bellow should each acknowledge a major debt to Twain. For *Huckleberry Finn* is the last great picaresque novel to be written by a white Anglo-Saxon American. The genre has been abandoned to the Negro and the Jew who, two generations from slavery or the *shtetl*, experiences for the first time and in full force what Ellison calls the magical fluidity of American life. A century after Hawthorne wrote *The Scarlet Letter,* our minority groups are re-enacting the central drama of that novel: the break with the institutions and authorities of the past and the emergence into an epoch of personal freedom and individual moral responsibility.

Ellison's revival of the picaresque reflects his group's belated access to the basic conditions of bourgeois existence. These consist economically of the freedom to rise and psychologically of "the right and opportunity to dilate, deepen, and enrich sensibility." The Southern Negro who is taught from childhood to "know his place" is denied these basic freedoms. He is deprived of individuality as thoroughly as any serf: "The pre-individualistic black community discourages individuality out of self-defense. . . . Within the ambit of the black family this takes the form of training the child away from curiosity and adventure, against reaching out for those activities lying beyond the borders."

The Great Migration of the Negro masses from Southern farm to Northern city was picaresque in character. In terms of Negro personality, it was like uncorking a bottle of champagne. Traditionally the journey has been made by railroad, and it is no accident that the blues are associated with freight yards, quick getaways and long journeys in "a side door Pullman car." No accident either that Ellison should emphasize his own wanderings: "To attempt to express that American experience which has carried one back and forth and up and down the land and across, and across again the great river, from freight train to Pullman car, from contact with slavery to contact with the world of advanced scholarship, art and science, is simply to burst such neatly understated forms of the novel asunder."

The bursting forth of Negro personality from the fixed boundaries of Southern life is Ellison's essential theme. And it is this, at bottom, that attracts him to the transcendentalists. For what was the central theme of Thoreau, Emerson and Whitman, if not the journeying forth of the soul? These writers were celebrating their emancipation from the Custom House, from the moral and political authority of old Europe. Their romantic individualism was a response to the new conditions created by the Revolution, conditions calling for *self*-government in both the political and moral sphere. Their passion for personal freedom, moreover, was balanced by a sense of personal responsibility for the future of democracy.

Ellison's debt to transcendentalism is manifold, but what is not acknowledged can easily be surmised. He is named, to begin with, for Ralph Waldo Emerson. In this connection he mentions two specific influences: the "Concord Hymn" and "Self-Reliance." The poem presumably inspires him with its willingness to die that one's children may be free; the essay, as we shall see, governs his attitude toward Negro culture. He admires Thoreau, plainly enough, for his stand on civil disobedience and his militant defense of John Brown. Whitman he finds congenial, for such poems as "The Open Road" and "Passage to India" are squarely in the picaresque tradition.

In broader terms, it may be said that Ellison's ontology derives from transcendentalism. One senses in his work an unseen reality behind the surfaces of things. Hence his fascination with guises and disguises, with the con man and the trickster. Hence the felt dichotomy between visible and invisible, public and private, actual and fictive modes of reality. His experience as a Negro no doubt reinforces his ironic awareness of "the joke that always lies between appearance and reality," and turns him toward an inner world that lies beyond the reach of insult or oppression. This world may be approached by means of the imagination; it is revealed during the transcendent moment in jazz or the epiphany in literature: *Transcend* is thus a crucial word in Ellison's aesthetic.

Above all, Ellison admires the transcendentalists for their active democratic faith. They were concerned not only with the slavery question but with the wider implications of cultural pluralism, with the mystery of the one and the many. To these writers, the national motto, *e pluribus unum*, was a serious philosophical concern. Emerson discerned a cosmic model for American democracy in the relationship of soul to Oversoul. Whitman, however, made the classic formulation:

> One's self I sing, a simple separate person,
> Yet utter the word Democracy, the word En-Masse.

Ellison reveals, in his choice of ancestors, the depth of his commitment to American ideals. When he describes jazz as "that embodiment of a superior democracy in which each individual cultivated his uniqueness and yet did not clash with his neighbors," he is affirming the central values of American civilization.

It remains to place Ellison in his twentieth-century tradition. What is involved is a rejection of the naturalistic novel and the philosophical assumptions on which it rests. From Ellison's allusions to certain of his contemporaries—to Stein and Hemingway, Joyce and Faulkner, Eliot and Yeats—one idea emerges with persistent force: *Man is the creator of his own reality.* If a culture shapes its artists, the converse is equally the case: "The American novel is in this sense a conquest of the frontier; as it describes our experience, it creates it." This turn toward subjectivity, this transcendence of determinism, this insistence on an existential freedom, is crucial to Ellison's conception of the artist. It finds concrete expression in his work through the devices of masking and naming.

Masking has its origin in the psychological circumstances of Southern life: "In the South the sensibilities of both blacks and whites are inhibited by the rigidly defined environment. For the Negro there is relative safety as long as the impulse toward individuality is suppressed." As soon, however, as this forbidden impulse seeks expression, an intolerable anxiety is aroused. Threatened by his own unfolding personality as much as by the whites, the Negro learns to camouflage, to dissimulate, to retreat behind a protective mask. There is magic in it: the mask is a means of warding off the vengeance of the gods.

Consider the jazz solo, one of the few means of self-expression permitted to the Southern Negro. Precisely because it is a solo, and the musician must go it alone, it represents potential danger. Ellison writes of certain jazz musicians: "While playing in ensemble, they carried themselves like college professors or high church deacons; when soloing they donned the comic mask." Louis Armstrong, as Ellison reminds us, has raised masking to the level of a fine art. Musical trickster, con man with a cornet, Elizabethan clown, "he takes liberties with kings, queens, and presidents." In a later development, the bearded mask of the bopster appeared, frankly expressive of hostility, rudeness and contempt. It is a pose which still finds favor among certain Negro writers of the younger generation.

In his own prose, Ellison employs various masking devices, including understatement, irony, *double-entendre* and calculated ambiguity. There is something deliberately elusive in his style, something secret and taunting, some instinctive avoidance of explicit statement which is close in spirit to the blues. His fascination with masquerade gives us two memorable characters in *Invisible Man*: the narrator's grandfather, whose mask of meekness conceals a stubborn resistance to white supremacy, and Rinehart, whom Ellison describes as "an American virtuoso of identity who thrives on chaos and swift change." A master

of disguise, Rinehart survives by manipulating the illusions of society, much in the tradition of Melville's Confidence Man, Twain's
Duke and Dauphin and Mann's Felix Krull.

Masking, which begins as a defensive gesture, becomes in Ellison's
hands a means of altering reality. For if reality is a process of becoming, that process can be partially controlled through manipulation of a ritual object or mask. "Masking," Ellison remarks, "is a play
upon possibility," and possibility is precisely the domain of art. To
clarify the matter he summons Yeats, a man not ignorant of masks:
"If we cannot imagine ourselves as different from what we are and
assume the second self, we cannot impose a discipline upon ourselves,
though we may accept one from others. Active virtue, as distinct from
the passive acceptance of a current code, is the wearing of a mask."
Yeats is speaking of morality, of active virtue, but the function of the
artist is implicit in his words. Before pursuing the point, however, we
must come to terms with a second feature of Ellison's art.

Naming likewise has its origin in negation, in the white man's hypocritical denial of his kinship ties. For the African slaves received from
their Christian masters not only European names but a massive in-
fusion of European blood, under circumstances so brutal and degrading as to have been virtually expunged from the national consciousness. At once guilty and proud, the white man has resorted
to a systematic *misnaming* in an effort to obscure his crime. Thus
the use of the matronymic to conceal the slave's paternity. Thus the
insulting epithets which deny not merely kinship but humanity. In
some obscene rite of exorcism, the white man says "nigger" when he
should say "cousin." And yet the family names persist as symbols of
that hidden truth, that broken connection which will have to be re-
stored before the nation, sick from the denial of reality, can regain
its mental health.

Having been misnamed by others, the American Negro has attempted from the first to define himself. This persistent effort at self-
definition is the animating principle of Negro culture. The earliest
appearance of Negro folklore, for example, "announced the Negro's
willingness to trust his own experience, his own sensibilities as to the
definition of reality, rather than allow his masters to define these
crucial matters for him." Similarly with musical expression: the jazzman who rejects classical technique is affirming his right to define himself in sound. Cultural autonomy, to Ellison, is an elementary act of
self-reliance. We have listened too long, he seems to say, to the courtly
Muses of white America. "Our names, being the gift of others, must
be made our own."

For personal as well as historical reasons, Ellison is fascinated by the
distinction between one's given and achieved identity. Named for a
famous poet, it was half a lifetime before he could define, let alone

accept, the burden of his given name. Acknowledging in retrospect the prescience of his father, he speaks of "the suggestive power of names and the magic involved in naming." We are dealing here with the ritual use of language, with the pressure which language can exert upon reality. This is the special province of the poet, and, broadly speaking, Ellison claims it as his own. He regards the novel as an act of ritual naming; the novelist, as a "moralist-designate" who *names* the central moral issues of his time.

"The poet," writes Ralph Waldo Emerson, "is the Namer or Language-maker." As such, he is the custodian of his language and the guarantor of its integrity. In performance of this function, Ellison has discovered that the language of contemporary America is in certain ways corrupt. "With all deliberate speed," for example, does not mean what it seems to mean when uttered by the Supreme Court of the United States. He proposes a rectification of the language and, therefore, of the nation's moral vision. For accurate naming is the writer's first responsibility: "In the myth, God gave man the task of naming the objects of the world; thus one of the functions of the poet is to insist upon a correspondence between words and ever-changing reality, between ideals and actualities."

As with naming, so with the image-making function as a whole. The artist, or image-maker, is guardian of the national iconography. And since the power of images for good or evil is immense, he bears an awesome responsibility. If his images are false, if there is no bridge between portrayal and event, no correspondence between the shadow and the act, then the emotional life of the nation is to that extent distorted, and its daily conduct is rendered ineffectual or even pathological. This is the effect of the anti-Negro stereotype, whether in song or statuary, novel or advertising copy, comic strip or film. Images, being ritual objects, or masks, may be manipulated by those who have a stake in the preservation of caste lines. What is required is a rectification of the nation's icons, a squaring of the shadow and the act.

Nor can this be accomplished through the use of counterstereotypes. Protest fiction, by portraying sociological types, holds its readers at a distance from the human person. But the problem is precisely one of identification. To identify, in the psychological sense, is to become one with. For this process to occur between white reader and Negro character, the writer must break through the outer crust of racial conflict to the inner core of common humanity. He must evoke, by his imaginative power, an act of "painful identification." To succeed requires the utmost in emotional maturity, craftsmanship and skill. For what the artist undertakes, in the last analysis, is the rectification of the human heart. . . .

Ralph Ellison's Modern Version of Brer Bear and Brer Rabbit in *Invisible Man*

by Floyd R. Horowitz

Mr. Ellison's Invisible Man is an intelligent, young Negro attuned to what he considers the clarion philosophy of the white world—"keep this nigger boy running." At first we find him like a bear, by his own admission, hibernating, unknown to anyone in a Harlem tenement basement. There he reflects upon his past experience, which soon, like Dante's travail to the blinding light of knowledge, is to be recounted. We can meanwhile understand symbolically one of his preoccupations. Around him in this dark basement he has rigged electric fixtures. He has tapped a power line and currently is stealing the electricity that illuminates his hibernation. On the ceiling and walls there are now 1369 lighted bulbs. Such enlightenment metaphorically sets the tone of the book. It is from one frame of reference a psychological study, impressionistically told.

So begins the story. In the South, once, a Negro boy was awarded by the whites a scholarship to a Negro state college. He was to learn the tradition of Booker T. Washington—practical service to the Negro community, humble dignity (at least in public), intellectualized acceptance of white authority. And naively on that foundation he frames his goals, and affixes in the rafters the hopeful branch of religion. Diligently and in innocence he learns to conform. As a reward, in his third year, he is chosen to chauffeur a visiting white trustee of the college.

The day is a disaster. Taking a back road he allows the delicately sensitive trustee to see the Negro in all his squalor. Following a conversation with a farmer who is known to have committed incest, the trustee faints and is carried to the only available haven, a saloon and

"Ralph Ellison's Modern Version of Brer Bear and Brer Rabbit in Invisible Man*"* *by Floyd R. Horowitz. From* Midcontinent American Studies Journal, *IV, No. 2 (1963), 21–27. Copyright © 1963 by the University of Kansas. Reprinted by permission of* Midcontinent American Studies Journal.

brothel just then at the height of its weekly business with the Negro ambulatory Vets of a mental institution. Within the day our hero is dismissed from the college of conformity, on the morrow traveling North to the expectation of greater freedom.

In short order, thus upon the verge of manhood, other disillusionments follow. The letters of recommendation which he carries from the college president prove treacherous. In the North he is economically exploited. Because of his skill as a public speaker he is enlisted by the Communists and later duped. In the shadow of each rebuff he distinguishes his grandfather's enigmatic smile and hears his words: "overcome 'em with yesses." Accordingly, the race of his experience in the South and North exhausts his consciousness of self. He finds that in running he is nowhere. Like a continually endangered Odysseus under the polyphemal white eye of society he is Noman. The whites are blind to him, he is invisible to himself, having failed in a succession of roles. While in itself this is a kind of knowledge by suffering, it is more than he can bear. His self-imposed basement exile is therefore an escape from responsibility, if also from the inequity of a hostile world. The winter of his discontent, he knows, must come to its hibernative end, and he must chance the new spring, yet for the time—and for the emphasis of the novel—his past disillusioning experience must be narrated.

Because the mode of that narration is impressionistic, Ellison takes the opportunity to convey the largest part of the novel's meaning via a quite imaginative, often bizarre range of imagery. In that way the logic of image associations sets out the basis of thematic implication. This may come as a new idea to the historian and litterateur alike, especially because the social and political significance of Mr. Ellison's book seems conclusively to derive from its open drama, colorful vignettes, and frank appraisals. Yet it may not be amiss to demonstrate that there is a good deal more social and political commentary being effected in the work via a highly planned if somewhat covert structure.

This means several things. Such a demonstration is necessarily involved with its own tools, the logic of interpolation as well as the more generally understood judgement of interpretation. Further, the story is not always told literally, but rather is rendered by symbols and images that have something like a life of their own. At an extreme (the Invisible Man's experience while in shock), the literal result takes the form of an impenetrable impressionistic morass, and the reader must agree to witness rather than to understand in the traditional sense. Other times a logical association can be drawn from similar instances: at the beginning of the novel the Invisible Man comes to a southern "smoker" where he will enter the prizefight ring, and while there he sees a nude dancer who has an American flag tattooed on her belly: at the end of the book he is described as a "black bruiser" who is "on the ropes" and "punch drunk," and he scrawls another distortion of another American message across the belly of another nude: "Sybil, you were raped/ by/ Santa Claus/ Surprise." Such devices as these form the texture (albeit an ironic one) of the American meanings which the hero experiences, and which no less importantly the reader is invited to experience with him.

As we do so we may trace the Invisible Man as a Christ-like figure, sacrificed and sacrificing. Many of the symbols by which he is described are distinctly Christian symbols, many of his actions are analogues of Biblical events. Or, psychologically considered, he is the dramatic vortex of Negro neuroticism: so extensive is the imagery here that we must read and interpret with the aid of an unabridged Freud. Historically and politically, too, he is beset by a cavalcade of American symbols and images which are in the wrong places, a sometimes subtle, sometimes raucous debunking of the names and institutions which Americans are supposed to hold so dear: the American flag upon her belly undulates to the shimmy of a nude, the identity of Jefferson is an illusion in the mind of a shellshocked veteran, the Statue of Liberty is obscured in fog while liberty is the name applied to a corporate enterprise, Emerson is a businessman, the Fourth of July is Jack the Communist's birthday as well as the occasion of a race riot.

Based fairly closely upon the folklore motif of Brer Rabbit and Brer Bear, the line of imagery discussed in this paper is as ironic as such other patterns of meaning, and perhaps even more so because of its Negro origin. Like the novel's fifty or perhaps seventy-five other motifs, it is not especially extensive, nor does it so closely effect an analogy that it admits of no other meaning for its individual parts. Quite the opposite. The bear and the rabbit are sometimes psychologically one and the same, as in Jack the Rabbit, Jack the Bear. But it would seem that the rabbit can be Peter as well. Or he is called Buckeye, which describes Jack the Communist later on. Or he is about to be peppered with BUCKshot. Or there is a pun on bear, so that the hero can not bear his existence. There is, in short, a rich language play which intertwines this motif with many others, which, perhaps too gratuitously on occasion, identifies rabbit with Brer Rabbit, which makes literary explication not the easiest of pursuits. Yet, for all that, the point of Ellison's use of this motif seems plain enough. Though they are sometimes friendly enough, less than kin and more than herbivorous quadrupeds, rabbit and bear are naturally irreconcilable. More, we know from Uncle Remus that soon they will match wits.

This makes for a good metaphor in which to cast the Invisible Man, since, interestingly enough, for Ellison, wit is not the same as intelligence. His protagonist is not a victor. Early in his education the Invisible Man discovers that. While he is chauffering Mr. Norton, the trustee of the college, they approach Jim Trueblood's backroad shack. The Invisible Man mentions that Trueblood has had relations with his own daughter. Norton demands that the car be stopped. He runs over to Trueblood, accosts him, wants his story. While the amazed and morally upright Invisible Man looks on, Trueblood complies in full detail. Ellison already has described him "as one who told the old stories with a sense of humor and a magic that made them come alive." And again, as one "who made high plaintively animal sounds." Now this story: sleeping three abed because of the extreme cold, his wife, daughter and himself, as if in a dream well beyond his control, just naturally, incest occurred. The story is a colloquial poetic. Before the act Trueblood has been nothing, but now he freely admits: "But what I don't understand is how I done the worst thing a man can do in his own family and 'stead of things gittin bad, they got better. The nigguhs up at the school don't like me, but the white folks treats me fine."

This irony is the key to Ellison's entire treatment of Brer Rabbit and Brer Bear's relationship. Here the issue is moral. Trueblood, in the middle of the night which he describes "Black as the middle of a bucket of tar," has given his daughter a baby. For this he is rewarded. Norton gives him a hundred-dollar bill. "You bastard," says the Invisible Man under his breath, "You no-good bastard! You get a hundred-dollar bill!" Playing the bear, the Invisible Man is fooled, of course; thrown out of school in a hurry. In vain he objects to the college president: "But I was only driving him, sir. I only stopped there after he ordered me to. . . ." "Ordered you?" retorts the president, "He *ordered* you. Dammit, white folk are always giving orders, it's a habit with them. Why didn't you make an excuse? Couldn't you say they had sickness—smallpox—or picked another cabin? Why that Trueblood shack? My God, boy! You're black and living in the South—did you forget how to lie?"

This is the form of the anecdote. Brer Bear is outwitted by Brer Rabbit in a first encounter. So the Invisible Man travels to the North. There on the streets of New York City he meets the second rabbit man, in this instance named Peter. Of course, exactly considered, Peter Rabbit is not the same as Brer Rabbit, yet he belongs to the same tradition. He knows how to escape the McGregors of the world. Here in Harlem he looks like a clown in baggy pants, wheeling a cart full of unused blue-prints. Says Peter, "Man, this Harlem ain't nothing but a bear's den." The Invisible Man then completes the bridge of logic to the original analogy: "I tried to think of some saying about bears to reply, but remembered only Jack the Rabbit, Jack the Bear." Peter needs no social reenforcement, however. He proffers his key to success: "All it takes to get along in this here man's town is a little shit, grit, and mother-wit. And man, I was bawn with all

three." So the friendly side of the rabbit's personality, advising the
Invisible Man what to expect from the city, the North, the white
world. But it is no use, for the bear must always be tricked—and
soon he is.

He has heard of a job at Liberty Paints and hurried to apply. The
scene depicts a patriotic devotion to the free enterprise system: flags
flutter from the building tops. A screaming eagle is the company's
trade mark. Liberty Paints covers America with what is advertised
as the whitest white possible, a defective shipment just then being
sent out for a Washington national monument. The bear is sent down,
down, down, to help the irascible Negro, Lucius Brockway.

"Three levels underground I pushed upon a heavy metal door
marked 'Danger' and descended into a noisy, dimly lit room. There
was something familiar about the fumes that filled the air and I had
just thought *pine,* when a high-pitched Negro voice rang out above
the machine sounds." In an image which we may recall, the first
rabbit, Trueblood, has already dreamed of such machinery. And
his black as tar description is taken up now by the Invisible Man's
thought of *pine,* and by Ellison's pun "high-pitched." So the hero
encounters Lucius, the next Brer Rabbit, who is described as small,
wiry, with cottony white hair, who defends himself by biting, and
whose coveralls covered by goo bring the image of the Tar Baby to
the Invisible Man's mind.

Against Lucius's grit and mother-wit there is barely any defense. It
turns out that Lucius alone has the secret of America's whitest white
paint. He and no one else knows the location of every pipe, switch,
cable and wire in the basement heart of the plant. Only he knows how
to keep the paint from bleeding (whereas Trueblood does actually
bleed for his moral smear), only he knows how to mix the base. He
has helped Sparland, the big boss, word the slogan "If it's Optic White,
It's the Right White." And he knows his worth: "caint a single doggone
drop of paint move out of the factory lessen it comes through Lucius
Brockway's hands." So in the matter of economics as before with
morals, Brer Bear can not win. As Lucius's assistant he tends the steam
valves, and when they pass the danger mark, burst, Brockway scrambles
for the door and escapes while the Invisible Man attempts to shut
them off and is caught in the steam. Again we may remind ourselves
that the concepts of machinery and scalding have been united in
Trueblood the rabbit's dream. Brer Bear can not win no matter how
hard he tries.

In this case, moreover, his efforts are naive, short of the hypocrisy
which alone means survival for the natively talented Negro. While
he struggles for consciousness and self in the company hospital, that
fact of Negro existence is brought out. A card is placed before him:
"What is your name?" Under the bludgeoning of experience he has

lost his identity, "I realized that I no longer knew my own name. I shut my eyes and shook my head with sorrow." The fantasy of his impression continues. Other cards are submitted, finally the question: "Boy, who was Brer Rabbit?" Soon after, he is released in a daze, finds his way to Harlem and collapses on the sidewalk.

Here Ellison has been portraying the New Negro intellectual. What has this Invisible Man learned?—that in the South, in the course of enlightenment he is pitted against his fellow Negro, farmer and college president alike; that Negro inured to the quasi-slavery practiced by the white. And in the North little better: survival in a slum, a bear in a bear den. Yet defeat is a realization, and a realization is a victory of perspective. In short, he is no simple Brer Bear. It is Ellison's intention to have him learn what the young intellectuals must learn—that as long as narrow self-interest motivates him he can have no peace. His must be the realm of the universal. That becomes the next phase, not with a rush of empathy, but as before, through trial, through defeat, through knowledge of self.

One day, when he has recovered from his ordeal in the paint factory, he comes upon the Harlem eviction of an aged Negro couple. Their meagre possessions on the sidewalk, the wife attempts to return into their apartment to pray. When the marshals in charge refuse permission the crowd riots. Suddenly in the melee the Invisible Man hears himself yelling, "Black men! Brothers! Black Brothers!" His further role as Brer Bear has begun. Under the aegis of his colloquial eloquence the crowd returns the furniture to the apartment. Then, in another moment, the police have arrived and he searches for a way of escape. A white girl standing in the doorway accosts him, "Brother, that was quite a speech you made," directs him to the roof. He hurries across to another building, down the stairs, into the street a block away, across to a far corner. But as he waits for the light to change there comes the quiet, penetrating voice beside his ear, "That was a masterful bit of persuasion, brother." The biggest, most persistent rabbit of all has just tracked him, Brer Jack the Communist, alias Buckeye the one-eyed international hopper. Brer Bear is wanted for the organization. Will he listen over coffee?

Says the Invisible Man, "I watched him going across the floor with a bouncy rolling step." Again: "His movements were those of a lively small animal." And Jack's pitch is short: "Perhaps you would be interested in working for us. We need a good speaker for this district. Someone who can articulate the grievances of the people. They exist, and when the cry of protest is sounded, there are those who will hear it and act." Communism is the answer to his needs, for as many reasons as it is advertised to have. It offers him a cause, social equality and a job. It fulfils what must seem the generic destiny of a Brer.

What informs the Communist policy is the scientific attitude, however, not the man but the mass. To this positivistic philosophy the Invisible Man must immediately be trained, for in the course of change to the new brotherhood, he is told by Hambro the Communist philosophe, certain sentimental ideas will have to be sacrificed. The very idea of race, that core and defense of Negro unity, must be sublimated. Nor is there place in the Brotherhood's teaching for emotion, for psalm singing, yam-eating, Tuskegee zeal. All is to be logical: the answers to the woman question, the rational youth groups, the organization of labor, even the public rallies. At least this is the theory, and if like Liberty Paints it is myopic and actually tinged with grey, if the women take him to bed to answer their political questions, if the youth are too easily frantic, if the public is still strong for the gospel and labor distrusts the Negro as scab; if these realities, the Invisible Man's idealism draws him into the bear trap, Brother Jack his foil.

His *is* a persuasive skill. Soon he is known, liked, trusted, powerful, confident that the Brotherhood is leading the Negro aright. Now he is willing to fight Ras the Exhorter, leader of the Negro-only movement. But as quickly, the trap springs: the internationally directed Brotherhood changes its Harlem policy. Indefinitely, there will be an interdiction of its plan to better the Negro's social condition. Unless the Invisible Man is willing to sacrifice the trust, the hopes of his fellow Negro, he must renounce identity once more.

In a scene which proves the Brotherhood's shortsightedness—Brer Jack, it turns out, actually has but one eye—there comes the break. But now, unallied, the Invisible Man must reckon with Ras the Destroyer, who in a Fourth of July flash electrifies Harlem as the nationalist leader of a super race riot. This is no time for intellectualism, nor this the place. Pursued, to survive, our hero has no choice but to hide in an underground cavern. There we find him when the novel begins: "Call me Jack-the-Bear, for I am in a state of hibernation." That is the pattern, from rural copse to cosmopolitan forest.

Irony From Underground—Satiric Elements in *Invisible Man*

by William J. Schafer

Although the term "black humor" has been pre-empted to describe a special form of modern comedy, it can be applied punningly to Ralph Ellison's comic elements in *Invisible Man*.[1] More accurate, however, is "black satire," again in a double sense; the novel's irony is at once representative of the Negro vision of comedy and of the grotesque, tragicomic vein of modern literature rooted in a sense of absurdity and existential crisis. Ellison summarizes the texture and feeling of black experience in America during the first half of the twentieth century. While the novel cannot be classified simply as comic, satiric irony is a major device of the story.

It is commonplace to note that Negro humor is at once a means of catharsis and a form of "code" communication. Wit and reflexive irony have been staples of Negro jokes, songs, and folk tales for centuries. During slavery times, comic tales formed a mythology for a largely illiterate and scattered captive culture; they provided a relief from suffering and degradation and a binding force or sense of identity for the blacks. While their experience was unalloyed tragedy, their escape from it was through the materials of comedy. Humor, in its simplest and most direct forms, pervaded black culture, developing from the language itself—arising from neologistic dialects and slang terms on through a rich and complex folklore still only partially appreciated. Humor permeated secular music, from field shouts and blues through party songs and jazz; all the forms of black music reveal acute wit and self-analysis.

Ellison has used all the resources of folk humor, black slang and the "underground" viewpoint of the Negro as his literary material. The imaginative synthesis of nonliterary attitudes and ideas is a

"Irony From Underground—Satiric Elements in Invisible Man" *by William J. Schafer.* From Satire Newsletter, *VII (Fall 1969), 22–28. Copyright © 1969 by William J. Schafer. Reprinted by permission of the author and* Satire Newsletter.

[1] All references to page numbers in parentheses are to the [Signet] paperback edition (New York, 1953).

testimonial to Ellison's skill in coping with a largely unexplored sub-culture. By using black language in a musical fashion and by trans-muting folk material into a literary vocabulary, Ellison created a work integrating the fearful complexities of Negro life with the ex-perience of modern white America.

Invisible Man is not strictly a satire, but Ellison creates satiric effects through extensive heavy irony. The structure of the novel is somewhat analogous to that of *Gulliver's Travels*; both works trace the adventures of an unsophisticated mind through a bewildering world of deceptive appearances, moving from comfortable innocence to desperate experience; both works rely on our sympathy with the protagonist-narrator; and both works rely on hyperbole and irony to create a symbolism for corruption and deceit in a complex society. But where Swift used the fantastic voyage pattern as a means of launch-ing a multi-levelled sociopolitical attack on the shibboleths of his age, Ellison works in the vein of the modern naturalistic novel. Fantasy is used mainly to create a nightmarish atmosphere overlaid on observed reality. And where Swift used obvious satiric allegory to veil the specific objects of his attack,[2] Ellison generalizes his irony to encompass a whole culture and its history. Furthermore, Ellison's major effect is not just that of satiric irony; much of the novel is psychologically realistic—it aims to convince the reader not of the existence of evil but of the feeling of injustice. The viewpoint is consistently that of the *victim*, and we are often less concerned with the details of white society's flaws than with their effects on a black mind and soul. The wry recognition of his existential dilemma gives the narrator a tone less like Swift's traveler or Dostoevski's Underground Man than like a blues singer carefully shaping a *double entendre*.

One main source of satiric irony is folk humor used as a meta-phorical description of Negro life. This takes several forms in *In-visible Man*. First there is the use of naive folk tales and folkways. When the invisible man is undergoing "reconstruction" after his first literally shattering encounter with the white industrial world, he is given a new identity. His white doctors help him to know who he is by recapitulating the folk history of his race. He becomes Buckeye the Rabbit, then Brer Rabbit, finally (by the end of the story) Jack-the-Bear—folk heroes and emblems of *survival* in the black world. These creatures cleverly outwit their enemies—white and black—and man-age not only to exist but to triumph. Mixed with this mythology is the old game of "playing the dozens"—a slanging match based on witti-cisms about your opponent's ancestry and legitimacy—"signifying"

---

[2] See Edward W. Rosenheim, Jr., *Swift and the Satirist's Art* (Chicago, 1963) and a very perceptive comment on this thesis, Gerald W. O'Connor, "Historical Criti-cism of Satire," *Satire Newsletter* VI (Fall 1968), 9-12.

or verbally outscoring an adversary.[3] The psychology of the satiric game here is clear and important. Ellison links this verbal duelling with the major theme of the novel—the quest for identity. To an oppressed person in a tradition of slavery, brutal one-way miscegenation and shattered families, the primal fears and jokes relate to the self and the family. Hence the power of the epithet "mother-fucker" in Negro invective. Hence the need for virile figures of strength and cunning like Jack-the-Bear. Patterns of survival in the novel often take the form of games or tests which require insight and ingenuity on the part of the protagonist/ It is a bitter joke that the white scientists with their electric womb and lobotomizing machine realize the invisible man's greatest weaknesses—"Why not a castration . . .?" one doctor ponders (p. 207). They have schematized his soul and mapped his mind, and they probe at the sores so clearly exposed.

So Ellison relates the unconscious patterns of folk humor to the Negro's greatest psychological and social traumas. From slanging matches and bawdy repartee come the revelations of the effect of centuries of white rape—physical and spiritual—on the black soul: "BOY, WHO WAS BRER RABBIT? He was your mother's back-door man, I thought" (p. 211). The language is that of the blues and the dirty joke and the sentiment that of sexual revenge, but the effect is to probe the basic materials of the black unconscious mind.

A second fund of satiric material comes from objects of everyday life—objects of scorn which Negroes associate either with oppression or with capitulation. Ellison skilfully weaves into the novel the folk mythology of the "down home nigger" and its rejection by urban sophisticates on the edge of the white world. "Soul food," the apparatus of skin-whitening, superstitions of the country mind—all are recorded as elements of black consciousness, elements which force a recognition of race on the narrator. When he is driven by despair and loneliness to eat a Carolina yam, associated with countrybumpkinism, the invisible man forces a sad pun, "I yam what I am" (p. 231). Later, a catalogue of the down home black's possessions reveals the facts of self-loathing forced on the black mind by a white world oriented toward social status and material wealth:

> . . . "knocking bones," used to accompany music at country dances, used in black-face minstrels . . . a straightening comb, switches of false hair, a curling iron . . . High John the Conqueror, the lucky stone . . . rock candy and camphor . . . . a small Ethiopian flag, a faded tintype of Abraham Lincoln. . . . In my hand I held three lapsed life insurance policies with perforated seals stamped "Void"; a yellowing newspaper portrait of a huge black man with the caption: MARCUS GARVEY

---

[3] This whole episode (pp. 209–11) is the best example of the way that Ellison integrates fantasy, naturalism and folk language into a single skein of logical action.

DEPORTED . . . . I read: FREE PAPERS. *Be it known to all men that my negro, Primus Provo, has been freed by me on this sixth day of August, 1859.* (pp. 235–37)

This pitiful junkheap is the material culture left the Negro in his corner of white America.

This relates to the narrator's state of mind in the prologue, when he is meditating on the meaning of the events he is to describe in the book. There, underground, he has come to grips with his culture and himself, and he bathes his soul in the despised fragments of the Negro's past:

> I'd like to hear five recordings of Louis Armstrong playing and singing "What Did I Do to Be So Black and Blue"—all at the same time. Sometimes now I listen to Louis while I have my favorite dessert of vanilla ice cream and sloe gin. I pour the red liquid over the white mound, watching it glisten and the vapor rising as Louis blends that military instrument into a beam of lyrical sound. (p. 11)

The humor of the narrator's self-recognition here, like most of that in the novel, is bittersweet and painful—the Negro is in the poignantly laughable position of being forced to repudiate the tatters of culture he has accumulated and is forced to stand like Lear's Poor Tom as "unaccommodated man," naked and helpless.

This reflexive satire is continued in Ellison's invention of Rinehart and Ras the Destroyer as poles of choice in the black world. Rinehart represents freedom without responsibility—he is duplicity, cunning, mere survival (like Brer Rabbit), seeming but not being, multiple identities, instability, flux and chaos. Ras—a caricature of Marcus Garvey's type of black nationalist—is one stable, undivided black identity, but it is one created of hate and violence, another form of chaos, ultimately as self-divisive and self-destructive as Rinehart's evasions. The invisible man's response to this dilemma is to evade the issue by literally dropping out of society and going underground. There is no choice in these two seeming opposites, and Ellison's satiric method is again close to that of Swift in Book IV of *Gulliver's Travels.* As Gulliver was presented with an impossible choice between inhuman rationality and unhuman irrationality and lost his reason in the confrontation, so the invisible man is shattered and driven to despair by his dilemma. The solution—if there is one—is left hanging at the end of the novel; there is no kindly, alleviating force like Captain Pedro de Mendez here to soften the harshness of Ellison's judgment.

Earlier uses of satiric caricature and disjunction have prepared us for this conclusion. At the beginning of the narrator's voyage from green southern innocence to sooty northern corruption, Ellision introduced a broad caricature of Tuskegee Institute, Booker T. Washington (the "Founder"), and the forces of nineteenth century rationalism and abolitionism. Bledsoe, the "Doctor Tom" president, and Norton, the "Old Marse" trustee, are monstrous twin images in the narrator's nightmare. Through them Ellison portrays the betrayal of black identity from the inside—Washington's ideal of humility ("live a humble life") is shown as a compound of obsequiousness and Machiavellian plotting (Brer Rabbit lurks inside this pose too), while Norton's patronizing missionary zeal turns into prurience and sexual delusion (he is obsessed with incest and lured by the familiar chimeras of Negro sexual license and prowess).

The "Brer Rabbit" philosophy of the narrator's past and culture— " 'Live with your head in the lion's mouth, I want you to overcome 'em with yeses, undermine 'em with grins, agree 'em to death and destruction, let 'em swoller you till they vomit or bust wide open.' " (pp. 19–20)—breaks down completely when the narrator reaches the white North. And in this portion of the novel we have Ellison's second major source of satire: the white world seen through black eyes. The first fund of material—the Negro's own mythology and stock of self-imagery—is directly connected with this, but Ellison uses the narrator's naivete and desperation as another distinct view of black and white cultures. While we see the black man enmeshed in his own absurdities (usually of white creation or perpetration), we also see the distinct effect of the "master" culture itself.

The first confrontation with white society takes the form of a nightmarish initiation ritual when the narrator is subjected to sadistic punishment by the white mandarins of his home town, then rewarded as a "good nigger" with a scholarship to college—a passport into the gelded black middle class. The whites are here cartooned as utterly corrupt—sexually depraved, drunken, oafish babbitts.

The second encounter is with a seemingly opposite type—Norton, the ancient abolitionist-oriented trustee, presumably the best of the nineteenth century traditions of philanthropy and altruism. He too is shown as inhuman, sexually disturbed, and treacherous. His tyranny is veneered with false generosity, but it is just under the surface; Norton's failure to comprehend the Machiavellian mind of Bledsoe, the college president, results in the narrator's expulsion from college and all his further wandering and torment.

The third revelation of white masks and white folly is through the character of young Emerson. In a scene involving parody of Ellison's namesake, Ralph Waldo Emerson, the narrator meets a young, neurotic liberal. Emerson espouses a chummy egalitarianism, complete with white-northern-liberal clichés (" 'Some of the finest people I know are Neg—' " [p. 167]), which turns out to be a thin disguise for sexual opportunism—Emerson is an invert trying on Leslie Fiedler's "solution" for black-white integration, homosexual misce-

genation. The confrontation, while brief, is pivotal in the novel—
Emerson drives the narrator from the tantalizing opulence of the
white middle class to the inferno of white industrialism. Liberalism
has proved another veil for corruption.

The fourth disillusionment is with white technology itself. The
episode at Liberty Paints discloses the falsity of the industrial world's
image; it is exposed as a hoax perpetrated by racists of both colors—
old Lucius Brockway is the image of the slave who works to keep
white society running. At the bowels of the industrial world is this
old slavery-time black whose goal is to keep the machines going
smoothly: " 'They got all this machinery, but that ain't everything;
we are the machines inside the machine' " (p. 190). Once more the
maze of the white world is revealed as Brer Rabbit's briar patch. Then
the narrator is betrayed and nearly destroyed by Brockway, who
leaves him to die in an exploding inferno.

The fifth disillusionment comes with the narrator's last recourse,
political radicalism. Brother Jack and the Brotherhood are revealed
also as duplicitous. The narrator, after an apprenticeship as a black
stooge, is expelled from the party when he thinks for himself; he
then meets Tod Clifton, another black figurehead also driven out,
selling black puppet-dolls in a symbolic revenge for his betrayal. The
masters have many guises, the last being that of radical egalitarianism,
in which the Negro is still a puppet, complete with nearly invisible
threads which make him dance his agonized buck-and-wing. The last
sociopolitical path to salvation is just one more dead-end street in
nigger heaven.

Other views of the white world used in Ellison's satiric vision in-
corporate powerful fantasies of Negro sexual prowess, which echo
through the story, and the delusion of "reconstruction"—the white
dream of neutralizing the black threat—which is a main theme. The
portrait of the white is of a fearful slave master who is at once fascinated by his captive and terrified of him, terrified to the point of
erecting elaborately disguised systems for duping and confusing the
black man. The white's attempts at love and understanding are constantly dissolving into lust and hatred. The invisibility metaphor which
controls the ideas of the novel is extended here to include the invisibility of the fences and fortifications of white America; it is a
basic variation on the central idea of most satire—the gross disparity
between *what seems to be* and *what is*.

The main feature of Ellison's satire in *Invisible Man* is its subtlety
and complexity. The irony of the book cuts both ways, and Ellison
is clear-sighted enough to portray failures and delusions of the Negro
as well as the grossly apparent sins of the white. The reflexive humor
is drawn mostly from folk humor and is buoyant and sustaining rather
than degrading. The jokes are wry seen from inside the castle of in-

visibility. Satire is traditionally a kind of minority report (often a minority of one), and Ellison distorts reality through caricature, fantasy, and hyperbole to show the *feelings* behind the facts of black existence.

He does this, in part, by allegorizing and parodying the facts of black history since slavery.[4] The novel recapitulates the Negro's experience since his (supposed) emancipation through a loosely picaresque framework. The narrator is as symbolic as the elements of his adventures and milieux, and we are asked (as in all satisfying satire) at once to sympathize with him and to view him critically. He is simultaneously fool and victim, and Ellison is able to project on his life the broad concepts which have shaped Negro attitudes—Washington's idea of success through service, Garvey's idea of black identity and solidarity, the influence of radicalism on the black mind, the cumulative impact of years of failure, misunderstanding, and confusion. The use of satiric allegory and irony allows Ellison to escape from the restrictions of naturalism and from the linear confinement of simple polemic. Because satire is based on criticism and attack, he can avoid merely arguing for a specific solution or expounding a limited viewpoint. It is this absence of the conventions and special pleading of the "Negro novel" pattern that gives *Invisible Man* its stature.[5]

The last major element of Ellison's satire is the hardest to describe concisely—the prose style which is the novel's musical foundation. It is a colloquial style, highly personalized yet capable of expository use, built on musical principles of rhythm and variation, swinging and loose like jazz itself. We are never far from the blues and the astringent humor of jazz in the novel. There are virtuoso performances and musical set-pieces as he imitates singing, jiving, and preaching, but the basic point here is that Ellison often uses this style for comic effects. He picks up jive rhythms and hip language, an effect like the surrealism of scat singing:

> "All it takes to get along in this here man's town is a little shit, grit and mother-wit. And man, I was bawn with all three. In fact, I'maseventh-sonofaseventhsonbawnwithacauloverbotheyesandraised onblackcatbones-highjohntheconquerorandgreasygreens. . . . You dig me daddy? . . . I'll verse you but I won't curse you—My name is Peter Wheatstraw, I'm the devil's only son-in-law, so roll 'em!" (p. 155)

He uses the descriptive powers of folk-storytelling graphically:

> "She screams and starts to pickin' up the first thing that comes to her hand and throwin' it. Some of them misses me and some of them hits me. Little things and big things. Somethin' cold and strong-stinkin'

[4] Richard Kostelanetz, "Invisible Man *as Symbolic History,*" *Chicago Review* 19 No. 2 (1967), 5–26.

[5] Marcus Klein, *After Alienation* (Cleveland, 1965), pp. 71–81.

hits me and wets me and bangs up against my head. Somethin' hits the wall—boom-a-loom-a-loom!—like a cannon ball, and I tries to cover up my head." (p. 59)

He constructs a polemical stump-speaking style out of West Indian dialect and the rhythmic shout of the down home preacher turned over to social themes:

"Don't deny you'self! It took a billion gallons of black blood to make you. Recognize you'self inside and you wan the kings among men! A mahn knows he's a mahn when he got not'ing, when he's naked—nobody have to tell him that. You six foot tall, mahn. You young and intelligent. You black and beautiful—don't let 'em tell you different!" (p. 324)

Finally, he uses simple fragments of daily speech in purely musical cadences:

"I wants all the women and chillun and the old and the sick folks brought out. And when you takes your buckets up the stairs I wants you to go clean to the top. I mean the *top!* And when you git there I want you to start using your flashlights in every room to make sure nobody gits left behind, then when you git 'em out start splashing coal oil. Then when you git it splashed I'm going to holler, and when I holler three times I want you to light them matches and git. After that it's every tub on its own black bottom!" (p. 472)

Ellison does not use simple invective as a satiric instrument, nor are his ironic points made directly, since his form is that of the naturalistic novel. The mind of the faceless narrator may be similar to Ellison's, but he is a distinctive personality, one like the controversial "masks" of traditional satire. But Ellison's humor and anger are projected through the language, and the characteristics of hyperbole and fantasy which shape the novel arise from the narrator's self-conscious manipulation of his language.

The final analysis of the black man's dilemma which Ellison offers is one shaped by irony and the power of satire to expose hidden truths but also shaped by a desire for a *solution* to the terrifying problems he describes:

. . . my world has become one of infinite possibilities. What a phrase—still it's a good phrase and a good view of life, and a man shouldn't accept any other; that much I've learned underground. Until some gang succeeds in putting the world in a strait jacket, its definition is possibility. Step outside the narrow borders of what men call reality and you step into chaos . . . or imagination. (p. 498)

Invisible Man charts the black man's perilous course between chaos and imagination. Along with the lash of satire, Ellison uses his capacity for understanding and empathy. While the answer to the invisible man's problems is not a simple one, and Ellison does not suggest a way out of our maze which does not have a cost, there is a clear feeling of the possibility of salvation at the end of the novel. The problem is shoved rudely into the reader's hands. The satiric attack of the novel is balanced, then, by an attempt to force the reader to analyze himself in the light of the invisible man's confessions. This combination of ironic exposure and analysis, in the end, makes *Invisible Man* the convincing drama that it is. We are left to decide whether this tragic farce will continue to play itself out or whether the forces of love and understanding can triumph.

The Symbolism of Vision

by *Charles I. Glicksberg*

The Negro novelist is under a severe handicap when he sits down to grapple with a specifically racial theme. How shall he embody it in a manner that is psychologically convincing and yet substantially true, without distorting the nature of his material? The temptation to sensationalize is in his case extremely strong: to indulge in the dynamics of violence, to dwell broodingly on such sadistic elements as beatings, brutality, hatred, murder, riots, lynchings, concentrated horror. Hence the Negro novelist is in search of a metaphor that will effectually carry his burden of meaning and "distance" the effects he is seeking to produce. If he resorts to the use of symbolism, it is because only in that way, by employing that expressive and infinitely resourceful medium, can he hope to convey some notion of the life that Negroes are forced to lead in the United States. The only question he must answer is, what symbol or set of symbols shall he weave into the warp and woof of his fiction?

For he is given a creative choice. The symbols he uses as well as the way in which he presents them will indicate the depth of his sensibility, the complexity and richness of his talent, the range and power of his vision. The symbol is not something artificially introduced, an alien and extraneous element arbitrarily imposed on the text. It is of the very substance and texture of fiction, inherent in language, an intrinsic part of the communicative and creative process. Vision is the heart of technique.

Endless are the possibilities and permutations of symbolism in a novel dealing with the Negro problem. The author, if he so wishes, may specialize in the symbolism of martyrdom: suffering, cruelty, punishment, aggression, sin and penance, blood and tears. Or he may view Negro life through the revealing perspective of the metaphor of flight: the fugitive, the hounded one, the fleeing victim. Or he may interpret his material, as Richard Wright does in *Native Son*, in terms of unrelieved horror (the symbolic cornering and killing of a rat in the open-

"The Symbolism of Vision" by *Charles I. Glicksberg. From* Southwest Review, *XXXIX (Summer 1954), 259–65. Copyright © 1954 by Southern Methodist University Press. Reprinted by permission of* Southwest Review *and the author.*

ing scene, the fight in the poolroom, the unpremeditated murder). Or he may attempt to view his problem experimentally through the multi-faceted and extraordinarily accommodating symbol of vision.

Ralph Ellison, in *Invisible Man*, relies heavily on the symbolism of vision: light, color, perception, sight, insight. These, his master symbols, are organically related to the dualism of black and white, the all-absorbing and bafflingly complex problem of identity. How does the Negro see himself and how do others see him? Do they notice him at all? Do they really see him as he is or do they behold a stereotype, a ghostly caricature, a traditionally accepted myth? What we get in this novel, creatively elaborated, is the drama of symbolic action, the language of the eyes, the incredibly complex and subtle symbolism of vision. All this is structurally bound up with the underlying theme of transformation. All this is imaginatively and, for the most part, success-fully worked out in terms of fiction.

What we get is a nightmare of delirium. Both the nightmare and the delirium are projected in sensory impressions of sight: lights turn on and off, red is the color of blood, white is the color of anger. The title itself is, in this respect, immediately suggestive: *Invisible Man*. Indeed, the "Prologue" states the central theme: the hero is invisible, not because he is constituted like the protagonist of the famous novel by H. G. Wells (from whom Ralph Ellison may originally have derived the idea), but because people refuse to see him. "When they approach me they see only my surroundings, themselves, or figments of their imagination—indeed, everything and anything except me." But this in-visibility is not peculiar to people of his color. The "vice" of vision resides in the eyes of the whites, who suffer not from a physiological disturbance but from a defect of their inner vision: "those eyes with which they look through their physical eyes upon reality." Here vision is tied up with the problem of reality. Perhaps the Negro exists or is real only as a phantom in other people's minds, like a figure in a night-mare that the sleeper struggles frantically to destroy.

Here, then, is a novel in which the symbolism of vision provides the dynamism and momentum of action, the motivational insight, the resolution of conflict. By virtue of his invisibility, the Negro is driven by the need to convince himself that he does exist in the real world, and he tries furiously to make others recognize his existence. When he attacks those who bump into him and who curse him, he realizes the futility of his murderous rage. What good does it do to lash out and slit the throat of an "enemy" who actually does not see him? How can a phantom strike back? What can an invisible man do to throw off the bondage of this blindness on the part of others, who are sleep-walkers?

The "Prologue" also describes how the protagonist carries on a fight with the electricity company, using their services without paying them a penny, draining the current free into the dark, dense jungle of Harlem. When he was visible he used to pay conscientiously for the privilege of light, but now that he is aware of his invisibility, he lives rent-free in a section of the basement of a building rented exclusively to whites. Here is the symbolism of a hole in the ground that provides an escape as well as a home, but the revealing thing about this hole is that it is flooded with light brighter than Broadway. The novel is charged with ironic contradictions of this kind. The hero, a nameless and symbolic figure, can now

> see the darkness of light. And I love light. Perhaps you'll think it strange that an invisible man should need light, desire light, love light. But maybe it is exactly because I *am* invisible. Light confirms my reality; gives birth to my form. . . . Without light I am not only invisible, but formless as well; and to be unaware of one's form is to live a death. I myself, after existing some twenty years, did not become alive until I discovered my invisibility.

That is why in his hole in the basement he floods the place with stolen electricity, determined to get more light. Invisibility proves an asset: it permits him to listen to music and understand its meaning, and it invests him with a different sense of time. Once when he smoked a reefer, he beheld visions of the past, Negro preachers eloquently discoursing on the text of the "Blackness of Blackness." That is the singular color obsession of the Negro, evident in his art, his songs, his religion, his literature. The "Prologue" emphasizes the nonexistence of the anonymous protagonist who leads a life of invisibility underground.

> Before that I lived in the darkness into which I was chased, but now I see. I've illuminated the blackness of my invisibility—and vice versa. And so I play the invisible music of my isolation. . . . Could this compulsion to put invisibility down in black and white be thus an urge to make music of invisibility?

But this state of invisibility will not last forever. Who can blame the Negro if at times he acts irresponsibly? Why should he assume responsibilities, social and legal, when the whites refuse to see him, to recognize his existence? To whom should he be responsible? "All dreamers and sleepwalkers must pay the price, and even the invisible victim is responsible for the fate of all."

The novel proper divides itself into two parts: in the first the hero plays the game according to the rules prescribed by the whites; in the second he rebels against the role forced on him, he fights back, he asserts himself. The nameless hero (since he is an invisible man he is bound to remain nameless) is no longer willing to accept the solutions that others offer, the answers that others furnish to the questions he asked. It takes him a long time to make the liberating discovery that he is nobody but himself.

While at college, the hero tries to do the right thing, to be a model student, but by repressing his emotions he snuffs out his essential humanity and loses his identity. He is the invisible man, negative, mechanical, anonymous. It is a mad doctor who reveals all the implications of the truth taught so unctuously to the Negro: white is right. But if one is to believe that and act on it, if obedience is to become automatic and instinctive, then blindness is absolutely necessary. The hero, in serving as the chauffeur of one of the rich, white beneficiaries of the Negro college, commits the unpardonable error of showing ugly and shocking aspects of Negro life that benevolent white philanthropists must never be permitted to see. The hero is asked to leave, but not before he has listened to a powerful sermon by a Negro speaker who is blind and has been told a number of blunt and bitter truths by the president of the college, a race leader who is enormously influential with the whites.

The hero takes the bus to New York, and in Harlem, a new world, the second chapter of his life begins. Armed with letters of introduction to white men from the all-powerful but treacherous president of the college which had expelled him, he sets out to redeem himself. He walks the streets, sits in the subway near whites, eats with them in the same cafeterias, and these novel experiences give him "the eerie, out-of-focus sensation of a dream." Though these people in New York are formally polite and even friendly, they hardly see him. When he realizes how he had been swindled by the scheming president of the Negro college, many things come into focus that he had formerly failed to perceive. Now he begins to search for his identity. He will no longer blind himself to the light of the truth. He gets a job in a plant in Long Island that manufactures "Optic White" paint, the best and purest white paint in the world. An old Negro worker has helped the owner make up the brilliant slogan: "If It's Optic White, It's the Right White," for which he receives a bonus. The hero observes the ironic humor of the situation: "If you're white, you're right," he says.

Invisible Man is a symphony of color contrasts, a study in the semantic refinements of vision, inner and outer. After an accident in the paint shop, the hero struggles to recapture his identity, to know his name. He asks himself: "Who am I?" Unfortunately he is lost in a jungle of blackness and pain. It occurs to him that perhaps identity and freedom are interconnected and interdependent. "When I discover who I am, I'll be free." The rest of the novel is the rapid-paced and fascinating story of his search for identity.

When he is released from the hospital after the accident, he comes face to face with the puzzling problem of his identity. When he returns to Harlem, he focuses dizzily upon the scene; he is undergoing a transformation, but he still does not know what to do with himself. "Who was I, how had I come to be?" He is finished with his past, filled with a wild resentment. He walks in a snowstorm, like a somnambulist. In one of the store windows of Harlem he sees some religious objects: Jesus and Mary and a black statue of a nude Nubian slave; another window contains ointments guaranteed to whiten black skin miraculously. Then, in the raging cold and snow, as he buys some yams from a vendor and eats them, he experiences an intense feeling of freedom. He no longer cares what the people who see him eating the yam will think. He would do what he liked. "I yam what I am!"

Then he is deeply moved by the sight of a Negro family being evicted in the midst of a snowstorm, and though he warns the crowd that has gathered against the use of violence he uses irony so devastatingly that a riot breaks out. As a result of this display of his capacity for leadership, he becomes involved with the Brotherhood: the Communist Party. Yet even here he feels invisible; even here color distinctions play a part. One woman in the Party would like him to be a bit blacker. The leaders of the Brotherhood look on him as a thing, an instrument. He is given a new name and is supposed to take on a new identity, but he does not yet know what that is to be. He is asked to address a huge protest meeting in Harlem, to function as a race leader. Perhaps the gaze of all the people in the audience will transform him, assure him of his identity.

On the platform he proves impassioned, irresistible, castigating his listeners for being so passive, so blind to their enslavement, their misery, their economic servitude. "We're a nation of one-eyed mice— Did you ever see such a sight in your life? Such an *un*-common sight!" And he vehemently bids them be careful not to lose their single eye or otherwise they will become blind as bats. Perhaps with both of their eyes properly focused they will be able to see their condition truly and recognize who is responsible for their terrible plight. He fiercely commands them to reclaim their sight, to combine and spread their vision. As he stands before them, the cynosure of all their eyes, he feels that he is becoming more human, more affirmative. "With your eyes upon me I feel that I've found my true family! My true people! My true country! I am a new citizen of the country of your vision, a native of your fraternal land."

Here is the man, spontaneous, full of vital feelings, transformed and transported, who would create the uncreated features of his race. "The conscience of a race is the gift of its individuals who see, evaluate, record. . . . We create the race by creating ourself and then to our great astonishment we will have created something far more important: We will have created a culture."

His activities as a worker for the Brotherhood prove most enlightening. He is pitted against the mighty prophet of Harlem, Ras the Exhorter, the demagogic exponent of black nationalism and Negro solidarity. Ras cannot stomach the Communist propaganda that stresses the ideal of all men united in brotherhood. For him blackness of skin is all, color is the badge of brotherhood, nothing else. Everything—politics, religion, God—is interpreted in terms of blackness: the holy color.

Gradually the hero, in his stormy odyssey of vision, comes to see that there are two sides of him: the old self and the new public self affiliated with the Brotherhood. When he organizes a public funeral, as a means of protest against the shooting down of a Negro by a white policeman, he seems to observe all that goes on as if he were a spectator: the tears, the shouts, the grief, the rage. Even here the symbol of vision predominates, and it adds a terrific sensory immediacy and intensity to the scene. The hero *sees* as well as acts.

When he is being arraigned by the Brotherhood for pursuing an ideologically incorrect course, he sees one of the leaders take his false eye out of his face and drop it into a glass of water, from which it stares up at the hero: "A buttermilk white eye distorted by the light rays. An eye staring fixedly at me from the dark waters of a well." But this mutilated leader is proud of the fact that he lost his eye in the line of duty. That is the price of loyalty, the meaning of discipline. Sacrifice, in short, involves blindness, and that is what Party discipline demands. Then the leader puts his false eye back in the socket and speculates about the new society that will provide him with a living eye. But what kind of society is it, the hero wonders, which will make the Communists recognize the existence of the Negro, see him as he really is?

Later, the hero, in order to escape from the clutches of Ras the Exhorter and his strong-armed followers, puts on dark glasses and is instantly plunged into blackness, barely able to see. He reads handbills put out by the Reverend Rinehart which speak of beholding the invisible, and in the church there are letters of gold on the wall: LET THERE BE LIGHT! At this point the search for identity is merged with the problem of what is reality. By coming North, the hero had jumped into the unknown. The dark glasses, however, have distinct potentialities; they can be used as a political instrument; they open up for him a new area of reality. The hero wants people to look at him. Wherever he turns, however, he encounters people, as among the Communists, who wish to sacrifice him for his own good.

The novel ends on a note of affirmative faith in the constructive potentialities of the Negro people. The Communist ideal is mechanical and merciless, without meaning or nourishing substance for the American Negro. The hero recognizes the nature of his fundamental contradiction: he *was* and yet he remained invisible. "I was and yet I was unseen." Suddenly all the disparate and confusing experiences of the past fall into place. He is the sum of his experiences. He had thought that the men of the Brotherhood accepted him because color was no criterion of brotherhood, when the truth was otherwise. The Communists didn't see color or complexion, men or individuals, only abstract principles, dynamic forces, historical movements, dialectical ideas. Every group tries to impose its version of reality, its visions and values, upon the Negro. But the hero, by accepting his invisibility, has grown in strength and stature. If he decides to remain invisible, it is because invisibility constitutes a potent source of protection.

The Party wanted him to ignore the unpredictable human element in Harlem, to portray the Negro masses as passive, pliable, receptive, to ignore the reality of their lives. Then comes the bloody riot in Harlem; the lights are shattered. It is then that he repudiates his connection with the Communists: he is no longer their brother; he is opposed to the strategy of fomenting class warfare which would mean race riots. Why should the blood of Negroes flow in the streets in order to further the interests of Communist propaganda? He has been running all his life; now Ras the Exhorter wants to kill him. But even if he were hanged by Ras matters would not be helped, for he would still remain invisible. He runs for his life and keeps running, unable to stop and explain—until he falls into a hole where he lies in the darkness upon black heaps of coal, and falls asleep.

When he wakes, he is still in the dark. There is no way out, no ladder, no ray of light. He burns everything he possesses, every scrap of paper that is connected with the past. Finally he comes to see that he must stop running; he must put an end to the illusions and lies of the past. He is now beginning to see, to understand. In destroying the Negro, the world is shedding its own blood. The nameless hero decides to remain underground.

In *Invisible Man*, Ralph Ellison projects his vision not only of the Negro people and its ambiguous existence, its metaphysically tormented existence, but also of life as a whole. In poignant and luminous symbolic terms, he pictures the fate of the Negro in America. As an invisible man (invisible precisely because of his high visibility), he is in a hole, but he is able to explore, to understand, to see the hole he is in, the trap in which he is caught. Out of this underground and invisible existence spring a number of profoundly painful problems. The Negro finds that distinctions between right and wrong, good and evil, are blurred and shifting. Then, too, there is a real risk in attempting to be himself, in viewing reality through the spectacles of the self. The Negro, in a society dominated by white values, cannot afford to be honest, to speak out freely. He must play a role of dissimulation, and conform to the white man's ideas and beliefs about the Negro. The original contribution of this novel lies in its symbolic reinforcement of the thesis that it is not enough to become and remain an invisible man.

What the suffering "hero" of this novel wants finally is the freedom not to run. The sickness, he perceives clairvoyantly, lies inside him.

Though the outer world was largely responsible for his condition, he was also guilty, and it is this burden of guilt that is viewed challengingly from different perspectives of symbolic vision. During his life underground the protagonist has learned that he is invisible, not blind. In his painful and protracted struggle to discover his true identity (and who in our time is not faced with this crucial task?), he perceives at last how he stands in relation to the world, with all the infinite possibilities of experience that this world holds out. He believes in diversity, not conformity. "Why, if they follow this conformity business they'll end up by forcing me, an invisible man, to become white, which is not a color but the lack of one." It is not colorlessness we want in this land, for life in America is richly multicultural, composed of many colors, textures, and patterns:

> Our fate is to become one, and yet many—This is not prophecy, but description. Thus one of the greatest jokes in the world is the spectacle of the whites busy escaping blackness and becoming blacker every day, and the blacks striving toward whiteness, becoming quite dull and gray. None of us seems to know who he is or where he's going.

Many may find that *Invisible Man*, complex in its novelistic structure, many-sided in its interpretation of the race problem, is not fully satisfying either as narrative or as ideology. Unlike the novel that depends for its appeal chiefly on the staple elements of love or sex, suspense and the dynamics of action, *Invisible Man* dispenses with the individualized hero and his erotic involvements, the working out of his personal destiny. Here we have, subtly and sensitively presented, what amounts to an allegory of the pilgrimage of a people: the dark, blood-stained story of the Negro's struggle to find himself, to rise to his full height as a man and achieve the glory of selfhood. Hence we must not rely on simple and specious solutions: the strategy of accommodation, however justified, or the dialectics of revolution. In order to solve his problem the Negro must cease to be invisible; but since he is not blind he must sharpen his vision so that he will be able to bring into proper focus the truth about himself. By means of the revealing master symbol of vision, Ralph Ellison has presented an aesthetically distanced and memorably vivid image of the life of the American Negro. To see: that is the preliminary and indispensable step on the part of the Negro people. Then they can set about liberating themselves from all the blind and mindless forces that keep them in dark bondage. The consistently effective use of symbolism, especially the symbolism of vision, in *Invisible Man* is no tour de force, no mechanically ingenious fictional device. It is a creatively original means for communicating the tragically ironic implications of the narrative, the meaning of the basic thesis that the true darkness, the worst darkness, dwells in the mind and heart of man.

Ralph Ellison and the
American Comic Tradition

by Earl H. Rovit

The most obvious comment one can make about Ralph Ellison's
Invisible Man is that it is a profoundly comic work. But the obvious
is not necessarily either simple or self-explanatory, and it seems to me
that the comic implications of Ellison's novel are elusive and provocative enough to warrant careful examination both in relation to the
total effect of the novel itself and the American cultural pattern from
which it derives. It is generally recognized that Ellison's novel is a
highly conscious attempt to embody a particular kind of experience—
the experience of the "outsider" (in this case, a Negro) who manages
to come to some sort of temporary acceptance, and thus, definition,
of his status in the universe; it is not so generally recognized that
Invisible Man is an integral link in a cumulative chain of great American creations, bearing an unmistakable brand of kinship to such seemingly incongruous works as *The Divinity School Address, Song of Myself, Moby Dick,* and *The Education of Henry Adams.* But the latter
proposition is, I think, at least as valid as the former, and unless it is
given proper recognition, a good deal of the value of the novel will be
ignored.

First it should be noted that Ellison's commitment to what Henry
James has termed "the American joke" has been thoroughly deliberate
and undisguised. Ellison once described penetratingly the ambiguous
locus of conflicting forces within which the American artist has had
always to work: "For the ex-colonials, the declaration of an American
identity meant the assumption of a mask, and it imposed not only
the discipline of national self-consciousness, it gave Americans an
ironic awareness of the joke that always lies between appearance and
reality, between the discontinuity of social tradition and that sense of
the past which clings to the mind. And perhaps even an awareness

"Ralph Ellison and the American Comic Tradition" by *Earl H. Rovit. From* Wis-
consin Studies in Contemporary Literature, *I, (Fall 1960) Copyright © 1960 by the
Regents of the University of Wisconsin, pp. 34–42. Reprinted by permission of the
Regents of the University of Wisconsin.*

of the joke that society is man's creation, not God's." This kind of ironic awareness may contain bitterness and may even become susceptible to the heavy shadow of despair, but the art which it produces has been ultimately comic. It will inevitably probe the masks of identity and value searching relentlessly for some deeper buried reality, but it will do this while accepting the fundamental necessity for masks and the impossibility of ever discovering an essential face beneath a mask. That is to say, this comic stance will accept with the same triumphant gesture both the basic absurdity of all attempts to impose meaning on the chaos of life, and the necessary converse of this, the ultimate significance of absurdity itself.

Ellison's *Invisible Man* is comic in this sense almost in spite of its overtly satirical interests and its excursions into the broadly farcical. Humorous as many of its episodes are in themselves—the surreal hysteria of the scene at the Golden Day, the hero's employment at the Liberty Paint Company, or the expert dissection of political entanglement in Harlem—these are the materials which clothe Ellison's joke and which, in turn, suggest the shape by which the joke can be comprehended. The pith of Ellison's comedy reverberates on a level much deeper than these incidents, and as in all true humor, the joke affirms and denies simultaneously—accepts and rejects with the same uncompromising passion, leaving not a self-cancelling neutralization of momentum, but a sphere of moral conquest, a humanized cone of light at the very heart of the heart of darkness. *Invisible Man*, as Ellison has needlessly insisted in rebuttal to those critics who would treat the novel as fictionalized sociology or as a dramatization of archetypal images, is an artist's attempt to create a *form*. And fortunately Ellison has been quite explicit in describing what he means by *form*; in specific reference to the improvisation of the jazz-musician he suggests that form represents "a definition of his identity: as an individual, as member of the collectivity, and as a link in the chain of tradition." But note that each of these definitions of identity must be individually exclusive and mutually contradictory on any logical terms. Because of its very pursuit after the uniqueness of individuality, the successful definition of an individual must define out the possibilities of generalization into "collectivity" or "tradition." But herein for Ellison in his embrace of a notion of fluid amorphous identity lies the real morality and humor in mankind's art and men's lives—neither of which have much respect for the laws of formal logic.

At one time during the novel when Ellison's protagonist is enthusiastically convinced that his membership in the Brotherhood is the only effective means to individual and social salvation, he recalls these words from a college lecture on Stephen Dedalus: "Stephen's problem, like ours, was not actually one of creating the uncreated conscience of his race, but of creating the *uncreated features of his face.*

Our task is that of making ourselves individuals. The conscience of a race is the gift of its individuals who see, evaluate, record. . . . We create the race by creating ourselves and then to our great astonishment we will have created something far more important: We will have created a culture. Why waste time creating a conscience for something that doesn't exist? For, you see, blood and skin do not think!" This is one of the most significant passages in the novel, and one which must be appreciated within the context of the total form if the subtle pressure of that form is to be adequately weighed. And this can be done only if the Prologue and the Epilogue are viewed as functional elements in the novel which set the tempo for its moral action and modulate ironically upon its emergent meanings.

The Prologue introduces the narrator in his underground hibernation musing upon the events of his life, eating vanilla ice-cream and sloe gin, listening to Louis Armstrong's recording, "What Did I Do to Be so Black and Blue?" and trying to wrest out of the confusions of his experiences some pattern of meaning and/or resilient core of identity. The next twenty-five chapters are a first-person narrative flashback which covers some twenty years of the protagonist's life ending with the beginning, the hero's descent into the underground hole. The concluding Epilogue picks up the tonal patterns of the Prologue, implies that both meaning and identity have been discovered, and dramatically forces a direct identification between the narrator and the reader. Ostensibly this is another novel of the initiation of a boy into manhood—a *Bildungsroman* in the episodic picaresque tradition. The advice of the literature teacher has been realized; the hero has created the features of his face from the malleable stuff of his experience. He who accepts himself as "invisible" has ironically achieved a concrete tangibility, while those characters in the novel who seemed to be "visible" and substantial men (Norton, Brother Jack, and even Tod Clifton) are discovered to be really "invisible" since they are self-imprisoned captives of their own capacities to see and be seen in stereotyped images. However, to read the novel in this way and to go no further is to miss the cream of the jest and the total significance of the whole form which pivots on the ironic fulcrum of the blues theme introduced in the Prologue and given resolution in the Epilogue. As in all seriously comic works the reader is left not with an answer, but with a challenging question—a question which soars beyond the novel on the unanswered notes of Armstrong's trumpet: "What did I do to be so black and blue?"

For the protagonist *is* finally and most comically *invisible* at the end of the novel; he has learned that to create the uncreated features of his face is at best a half-value, and at worst, potentially more self-destructive than not to strive after identity at all. For Ellison ours is a time when "you prepare a face to meet the faces that you meet"—

a time when we have learned to shuffle and deal our personalities with a protean dexterity that, as is characterized through Rinehart, is a wholesale exploitation of and surrender to chaos. After the narrator's fall into the coalpit he discovers that his arrogantly naive construction of personality is nothing more than the accumulated fragments in his briefcase: the high-school diploma, Bledsoe's letter, Clifton's dancing doll, Mary's bank, Brother Tarp's iron. And most ironically, even these meager artifacts—the fragments he has shored against his ruin —represent not him, but the world's variegated projections of him. The narrator learns then that his educational romance is a farcical melodrama of the most garish variety; the successive births and re-births of his life (his Caesarean delivery from college, his birth by electronics at the factory hospital, the christening by the Brotherhood) were not the organic gestations of personality that he idealized so much as they were the cold manipulations of artificial insemination. His final acceptance of his invisibility reminds us of the demand of the Zen Master: "Show me the face you had before you were born."

However, we must note also that this acceptance of invisibility, of amorphous non-identity, is far from a resignation to chaos. The protagonist has successfully rebelled against the imposition of social masks whether externally (like Clifton's) or internally (like Brother Tarp's) bestowed; his is not a surrender of personality so much as a descent to a deeper level of personality where the accent is heavier on possibilities than on limitations. The 1,369 glowing light bulbs in his cellar retreat attest to the increased power and enlightenment which are positive gains from his experience, as well as to the strategic advantages of his recourse to invisibility. The literature teacher un-wittingly pointed out the flaw in his exhortation even as he declaimed it: "Blood and skin do not think!" For to think is to be as much con-cerned with analysis as it is with synthesis; the ironic mind tears radi-ant unities apart even as it forges them. Accordingly Ellison's narrator assumes the ultimate mask of facelessness and emphasizes the fluid chaos which is the secret substance of form, the dynamic interplay of possibilities which creates limitations. The narrator is backed into the blank corner where he must realize that "the mind that has con-ceived a plan of living must never lose sight of the chaos against which that pattern was conceived." In accepting himself as the Invisible Man he assumes the historic role which Emerson unerringly assigned to the American poet; he becomes "the world's eye"—something through which one sees, even though it cannot itself be seen.

And here it may be fruitful to investigate briefly the peculiar rela-tionship of Emerson's work to Ellison (whose middle name is pro-pitiously Waldo). In the recently published excerpt from a novel in progress, "And Hickman Arrives," Ellison has his main character, Alonzo Zuber, Daddy Hickman, make some complimentary remarks about Emerson, "a preacher . . . who knew that every tub has to sit on its own bottom." Daddy Hickman, a Negro preacher ("Better known as GOD'S TROMBONE"), is vividly characterized as a wise and shrewd virtuoso of the evangelical circuit who might not unfairly be taken as a modern-day Emerson, preaching eloquently the gospel of humanity. These facts may be significant when we remember that Emerson's work is given short shrift as rhetorical nonsense in *Invisible Man* and his name is bestowed upon a character whose minor function in the novel is to be a self-righteous hypocrite. This shift in attitude may indicate that Ellison has come to realize that there are some major affinities binding him to his famous namesake, and, more important, it may enable us to understand more clearly the remarkable consistency of the American struggle to create art and the relatively harmonious visions which these unique struggles have attained.

Superficially there would seem to be little to link the two men beyond the somewhat labored pun of their names and Ellison's awareness of the pun. The one, an ex-Unitarian minister of respectable, if modest, Yankee background, whose orotund explorations in autobiography gave fullest form to the American dream—whose public pose attained an Olympian serenity and optimistic faith which have caused him to be associated with a wide range of sentimentalities from Mary Baker Eddy to Norman Vincent Peale; the other, an Oklahoma City Negro, born in 1914, ex-Leftist propagandist and editor, who would seem to have belied the Emersonian prophecy of individualism and self-reliance by the very title of his novel, *Invisible Man*. The one, nurtured by the most classical education that America had to offer; the other, a rapt disciple of jazzmen like Charlie Christian and Jimmy Rushing who has attributed to their lyric improvisations his deepest understanding of aesthetic form. The one, white and given to the Delphic utterance; the other, black and adept in the cautery of bitter humor. But in their respective searches for identity, in their mutual concern with defining the possibilities and limitations which give form and shape to that which is human, the poet who called man "a golden impossibility" and the novelist who teaches his protagonist that life is a latent hive of infinite possibilities draw close together in their attempts to find an artistic resolution of the contrarieties of existence.

"Only he can give, who has," wrote Emerson; "he only can create, who is." Experience is the fluxional material from which these all-important values and identities are created, and Emerson's great essays are processive incantations whose ultimate function is to bring identity into being, even as they chant the fundamental fluidity of all forms spontaneously and eternally merging into other forms. When we remember that Emerson once wrote: "A believer in Unity, a seer of Unity, I yet behold two," it may be worth a speculation that the Emerson behind the triumphant artifices of the *Essays* was not a terribly different person from the Invisible Man in the coalpit whose submersion into the lower frequencies had given him an entree to the consciousnesses of all men. This awareness of the absurdity of meaning (and the potential meaningfulness of chaos) is at the heart of Emerson's delight in paradox, his seeming inconsistencies, his "dialogistic" techniques, his highly functional approach to language. "All symbols are fluxional," he declaimed; "all language is vehicular and transitive and is good for conveyance not for homestead." Thus Melville's attempted criticism of Emerson in *The Confidence Man* misses widely the mark; Emerson isn't there when the satire strikes home. Melville, who above all of Emerson's contemporaries should have known better, mistook the Olympian pasteboard mask for a reality and misread the eloquent quest for identity as a pretentious melodrama. For, as Constance Rourke recognized, Emerson is one of our most deft practitioners of the American joke, and the magnitude of his success may be measured by the continued effectiveness of his disguises after more than a hundred years.

But again we must return to the *form* of *Invisible Man* to appreciate how deeply involved Ellison's work is with the most basic American vision of reality. Although it is probably true as some critics have pointed out that the dominating metaphor of the novel—the "underground man" theme—was suggested by Dostoevsky and Richard Wright, it is for our purposes more interesting to note a similar metaphor in Hart Crane's poem, "Black Tambourine":

> The interests of a black man in a cellar
> Mark tardy judgment on the world's closed door.
> Gnats toss in the shadow of a bottle,
> And a roach spans a crevice in the floor.
> . . . .
>
> The black man, forlorn in the cellar,
> Wanders in some mid-kingdom, dark, that lies,
> Between his tambourine, stuck on the wall,
> And, in Africa, a carcass quick with flies.

Invisible Man achieves an expert evocation of that "mid-kingdom," that *demi-monde* of constant metamorphosis where good and evil, appearance and reality, pattern and chaos are continually shifting their shapes even as the eye strains to focus and the imagination to comprehend. The Kafkaesque surrealism of the novel's action, the thematic entwinement of black-white and dark-light, and the psychic distance from the plot-development which the use of the Prologue and the Epilogue achieves posit the moral center of the novel in that fluid area where experience is in the very process of being transformed into value. The narrator, the author, and the reader as well are caught in the "mid-kingdom" which seems to me to be the characteristic and unavoidable focus of American literature. For this mid-kingdom, this unutterable silence which is "zero at the bone," seems to me to be the one really inalienable birthright of being an American. Some Americans following Swedenborg named it "vastation"; others gave it no name and lamented the dearth of an American tradition within which the artist could work; at least one commissioned the sculptor Saint-Gaudens to incarnate it in a statue. One way of attempting to describe the sense of being within this mid-kingdom can be most dramatically seen in "The Castaway" chapter of *Moby Dick* where Pip is left floundering in the boundless Pacific. And although the techniques of approaching the experience have been richly various, the experience itself, an incontrovertible sense of absolute metaphysical isolation, can be found at the core of the most vital American creations.

"American history," writes James Baldwin in *Notes of a Native Son*, is "the history of the total, and willing, alienation of entire peoples from their forebears. What is overwhelmingly clear . . . is that this history has created an entirely unprecedented people, with a unique and individual past." The alienation, of course, is more than sociological and ideological; it seeps down into the very depths whence the sureties of identity and value are wrought; and it imprisons the American in this mid-kingdom where the boundaries—the distance from the tambourine on the wall to the carcass quick with flies—cannot be measured in either years or miles. The American seeking himself—as an individual, a member of the collectivity, a link in the chain of tradition—can never discover or create that identity in fixed restrictive terms. The past is dead and yet it lives: note Ellison's use of the narrator's grandfather, the yams, the techniques of the evangelical sermon. Individuals are frozen in mute isolation, and yet communication is possible between them: the Harlem riot, the way the narrator listens to music. Ellison's novel is the unique metaphor of his own thoroughly personal experience, and yet it makes a fitting link in the chain of the American tradition.

That Ellison and his narrator are Negroes both is and is not important. From the severe standpoint of art the racial fact is negligible, although there are doubtless areas of meaning and influence in *Invisible Man* which sociological examination might fruitfully develop. From the viewpoint of cultural history, however, the racial fact is enormously provocative. It is strikingly clear that contemporary American writing, particularly the writing of fiction, is dominated by two categories of writers: members of religious and racial minorities, and writers who possess powerful regional heritages. Both groups have an instinctive leasehold within the boundaries of the "mid-kingdom"; the Negro, the Catholic, the Jew, and the Southerner share the immediate experience of living on the razor's edge of time, at the very point where traditions come into desperate conflict with the human need to adapt to change. And, of equal importance, both groups—in varying degrees—are marked out on the contemporary scene as being "different"; both groups cannot avoid the terrible problem of identity, because it is ever thrust upon them whether they like it or not. These are the conditions which in the American past have nourished our spasmodic exfoliations of significant literary activity: the great "Renaissance" of the 1840's and '50's, the Twain-James-Adams "alliance" of the late nineteenth century, the post-World War One literary florescence from which we have just begun to break away. But the Lost Generation was the last generation which could practise the necessary expatriation or "fugitivism" in which these factors—the disseverance from the past and the search for identity—could operate on non-minority or non-regional American writers. Thus Ralph Ellison— and contemporaries like Saul Bellow, Flannery O'Connor, and William Styron—are *inside* the heart of the American experience by the very virtue of their being in some way "outsiders." Like Emerson, himself a royal inhabitant of the mid-kingdom over a century ago, they are challenged to create form, or else succumb to the enveloping chaos within and without.

And the answers which they arrive at—again as with Emerson— are answers which cannot be taken out of the context of their individually achieved forms without being reduced to platitude or nonsense. Form, the creation of a radical, self-defining metaphor, is the one rational technique which human beings have developed to deal adequately with the basic irrationality of existence. The answer which *Invisible Man* gives to the unanswerable demands which life imposes on the human being has something to do with human limitation and a good deal to do with freedom; it has something to do with hatred, and a good deal more to do with love. It defines the human distance between the tambourine and the carcass and it accepts with wonder and dignity the immeasurable gift of life. The black man in the cellar transforms his isolation into elevation without denying the brute facts of existence and without losing his ironic grip on the transiency of the moment. The amorphous ambiguity of the mid-kingdom is for a timeless instant conquered and made fit for habitation. Perhaps tragedy teaches man to become divine, but before man can aspire to divinity, he must first accept completely the responsibilities and limitations of being human. The American experience, cutting away the bonds of tradition which assure man of his humanity, has not allowed a tragic art to develop. But there has developed a rich and vigorous comic tradition to which *Invisible Man* is a welcome embellishment, and it is this art which promises most as a healthy direction into the future.

The American Negro and the
Image of the Absurd

by Esther Merle Jackson

One of the factors affecting the changing status of the American
Negro today is the rise of certain new perspectives which have altered
our perception of the condition of man. The modern arts, in particular
the art of literature, have dramatized the fact that an ever larger seg-
ment of humanity seems to share the kind of existence which has been
the lot of the Negro for some three centuries or more. The shape of
human suffering, defined by Dostoevsky, Proust, Gide, Malraux, Mann,
Sartre, and others, mirrors the actual condition of the Negro: his alienation from the larger community, his isolation within abstract walls, his
loss of freedom, and his legacy of despair. Although many modern
writers trace their vision of the human dilemma to developments in
European intellectual history, it is quite clear that one of the percep-
tions profoundly affecting the modern mind has been the image of the
Negro. Indeed, it may be said that he has served as a prototype of that
contemporary philosophic species, "the absurd." [1]

But the image of man as the absurd is not new. For the absurd
sensibility is an acute consciousness of human crisis: it celebrates man's
desperate struggle to order the moral universe, without recourse to
powers outside of himself. Like all symbols, the image of man as the
absurd has had an extended aesthetic and philosophic history. Characteristic aspects of this perception may be seen throughout Western literature: in the work of Aeschylus, Euripides, Shakespeare, Cervantes,
Milton, Molière, and Goethe, among others. Albert Camus, in his catalogue of heroes, cites Quixote, Hamlet, and Don Juan, along with
Sisyphus, Prometheus, and Jesus Christ. While certain components of
this radical perception appear in earlier forms of literature, philosophy,

"The American Negro and the Image of the Absurd" by Esther Merle Jackson.
From Phylon, XXIII (Winter 1962), 359–71. Copyright © 1962 by Atlanta University. Reprinted by permission of Phylon.

The original article develops the theme of the absurd in Faulkner and Wright as
it leads up to Ellison's conception. The omissions are indicated by ellipses.

[1] Albert Camus, The Myth of Sisyphus, trans. Justin O'Brien (New York, 1955).

and theology, the actual elevation of man to the plane of ultimate power and responsibility in and for the world is, in the main, the contribution of the contemporaries. The modern perspective begins, writes Camus, at the moment when Dostoevsky's Raskolnikov declares that "everything is possible." It is this universe of infinite human possibility that Camus and others have named "the absurd."

It is, perhaps, fitting that the American Negro should stand as a symbol, a sign, of the total condition of man in the twentieth century. For in many ways, the Negro is the very ground of the human conflict in our time. Like America itself, he may be described as a *synthesis,* as an attempt to reconcile certain antithetical ideas embodied in the terms: Europe and Africa, black and white, master and slave. But the fundamental absurdity of his condition—like that of modern man in general—may be traced to an even more critical ideological encounter: to the tension arising from the collision between the ethic of power and the idea of moral law. It is this moral crisis—the culmination of a long historical struggle—which engages the mind of our epoch; its implications extend far beyond the projected solution of the Negro's immediate problem to the question of human survival on this planet.

American literature has always reflected an interest in the idea of a responsible humanity. European writers of the twentieth century are heavily indebted to the American Classicists, Hawthorne, Emerson, Whitman, Melville, and O'Neill, as well as to more contemporary-minded artists such as Poe, James, Faulkner, Wright, Steinbeck, Hemingway, and others. While no one of these, with the possible exception of O'Neill, has been consciously concerned with the idea of the Negro as the absurd, there have been suggestions of this theme in the work of many less popular artists, particularly in that of Negro writers such as Langston Hughes. In the main, however, the image of the Negro as hero in American literature is fragmentary. We may, however, piece together a vision of his role in the moral universe, from partialities. Three such component visions are William Faulkner's *Light in August,* Richard Wright's *Native Son,* and Ralph Ellison's *Invisible Man.* While these works have, formerly, been interpreted in light of other critical perspectives, they may now be read as studies in phases of the absurd sensibility. Together, they compose an anti-traditional image of the Negro. For they may be read as a composite chronicle of his journey toward understanding, knowledge, and responsibility, in the climate of the absurd.

Absurd Walls

Albert Camus writes that the most crucial of all considerations in the climate of the absurd is man's reflection upon the significance of his own life. Indeed, this is the beginning of the cycle of heroic action, the initial gesture toward responsibility, freedom, and knowledge: "I therefore conclude that the meaning of life is the most urgent of all questions. How to answer it?" The absurd is that kind of man who wills to discover—or to impose—meaning upon an existence for which he has been able to determine no real purpose:

> What, then, is that incalculable feeling that deprives the mind of the sleep necessary to life? A world that can be explained even with bad reasons is a familiar world. But, on the other hand, in a universe suddenly divested of illusions and lights, man feels an alien, a stranger. His exile is without remedy since he is deprived of the memory of a lost home or the hope of a promised land. This divorce between man and his life, the actor and his setting, is properly the feeling of absurdity.[2]

Such a figure is Joe Christmas, the protagonist of William Faulkner's *Light in August*. Christmas, like Camus' Sisyphus, is the apparition of "the outsider." He is a metaphysical prisoner, a man trapped between concepts called "black" and "white." . . .

We may describe this ritual sufferer in terms of our contemporary metaphor as absurd, for he belongs to no distinct order of beings. He has been denied the black plane of reality without having been accepted in the white world of tragic meaning. He is condemned to suffer behind the walls of a wasteland: a world of nothingness. He is, in the language of T. S. Eliot, "Caught in the form of limitation. Between un-being and being." [3]

. . . *Light in August* may be seen, as an effective account of the initial phase in the cycle of absurd consciousness, as a record of a human crisis behind absurd walls. Faulkner, a Southern writer, interprets this critical moment in the life of a man in terms of his myth of color. Joe Christmas, like Camus' Meursault or Kafka's Joseph K, may be read as an image of modern man in search of understanding, in desperate need of a structure through which he may escape the meaninglessness of his life.

Absurd Revolt

If Willim Faulkner's *Light in August* provides an effective image of a Negro as an absurd sufferer, Richard Wright's *Native Son* is, perhaps, to this time, the most moving and passion-filled portrait of a Negro as man in revolt against Fate.[4] Interpreted in the forties primarily as a socio-political tract, *Native Son* may in the light of recent

[2] *Ibid.,* p. 6.

[3] Thomas Stearns Eliot, "Burnt Norton," *Four Quartets* (New York, 1943), p. 8.

[4] Revolt is one theme of the discussion of *Native Son* in Morris Weitz, *A Philosophy of the Arts* (Cambridge, Massachusetts, 1950), pp. 137–41.

history—political and intellectual—be seen for its greater merit: as a record of a man's dramatic encounter with Fate in the climate of the absurd. To be understood clearly, *Native Son* should be viewed in the light of other works in the contemporary *genre*. Like *Crime and Punishment*, or *The Stranger*, it is a study in the second phase of the absurd cycle—revolt. It is the chronicle of a terror-filled and terrifying search for a way to escape the absurd walls.[5]

Although Bigger Thomas is like Joe Christmas in the essentials of the dilemma he endures, he differs from Faulkner's protagonist in ways which are, perhaps, to be expected. For Wright seems to understand the internal life of his character more clearly, and is thus able to give him richer motivation. Bigger's complexity connotes his advance in consciousness over that of the earlier protagonist. Like Hamlet, he not only feels his dilemma, he understands it. He perceives his role, his alienation from the two worlds which compose the absurd universe. . . .

In the early moments of the novel, he sees himself as a victim of this struggle, as a man caught in the lines of force between that power represented by the "white" world and that servility embodied in the "black." Like Christmas, Bigger sees himself as a creature deprived of being:

> To Bigger and his kind, white people were not really people; they were a sort of great natural force, like a stormy sky looming overhead; or like a deep swirling river stretching suddenly at one's feet in the dark. As long as he and his black folks did not go beyond certain limits, there was no need to fear that white force. But whether they feared it or not, each and every day of their lives they lived with it; even when words did not sound its name, they acknowledged its reality.[6]

Bigger, like Hamlet, broods upon his dilemma. Similarly, he seeks to amend his fate by choosing to identify himself with that idea which he believes to have been the genesis of his suffering. He elects power as the sign of his being. It is important at this point to remember that *Native Son* was written in the thirties, at a time when the question which confronted Bigger Thomas absorbed the world consciousness. Bigger Thomas, child of his age, chooses to join the cult of the Nietzschean "superman." He elects violence, crime, and vengeance as the signs of life. *Native Son* has, then, certain significant elements of the more conventional tragic vision, especially of Aeschylean form. For Bigger, like his modern European counterpart, echoes the Promethean, the metaphysical criminal, in revolt against established law. *Native Son* is the chronicle of a man's collision with Fate, in the climate of the absurd.

[5] See Robert A. Bone, *The Negro Novel in America* (New Haven, 1958), p. 144.
[6] Richard Wright, *Native Son* (New York, 1940), p. 97.

. . . It is for Bigger, then, as it has always been for the hero, . . .
consciousness of guilt which is the access to knowledge. Through his
cycle of suffering and revolt, he comes at last to a passion for life itself,
to the threshold of meaning:

"I ain't trying to forgive nobody and I ain't asking for nobody to forgive me. I ain't going to cry. They wouldn't let me live and I killed.
Maybe it ain't fair to kill, and I reckon I didn't really want to kill. But
when I think of what all the killing was, I begin to feel what I wanted,
what I am. . . ."

. . . .

"I didn't want to kill!" Bigger shouted. "But what I killed for, I am!
It must have been pretty deep in me to make me kill! I must have felt it
awful hard to murder. . . ."

. . . .

"What I killed for must've been good!" Bigger's voice was full of frenzied anguish. "It must have been good! When a man kills, it's for something. . . . I didn't know I was really alive in this world until I felt
things hard enough to kill for 'em. . . . It's the truth, Mr. Max. I can
say it now, 'cause I'm going to die. . . ." [7]

Absurd Freedom

Wright poses, but does not clearly answer, the critical question as
it affects his protagonist in the climate of the absurd: What are the
conditions of heroism in the modern world? What is the actual nature
of the freedom which modern man seeks? It is to this question that the
last, and in many senses most important, of these works is directed.
Indeed, perhaps the only novel which seems to be consciously concerned with discovering an answer to this question as it affects the
American Negro is Ralph Ellison's distinguished work, *Invisible Man*.
This novel shows, of course, many correspondences to the contemporary European form of Malraux, Sartre, Camus, and others. The novel,
like the work of the Europeans cited, is the imitation of a search for
intellectual clarity and order. *Invisible Man* recapitulates the odyssey of
the philosophic "I," the journey of the fragmentary self through
experience to knowledge and, ultimately, to being.

Invisible Man may be described as a philosophical novel; that is to
say, its major interest lies in the illumination of, if not the answer to,
the question of the human freedom. Ellison's work differs in certain significant ways from that of both Wright and Faulkner. To begin with,
the novelist endows his protagonist with a higher level of consciousness
than that of Christmas or of Bigger. For Ellison's protagonist is not

[7] Wright, *Native Son*, p. 358.

only the "I" of experience; he is also the reasoning "I," the thinking self in search of a mode of reconciliation in which all of the conflicts present in existence may be unified. Ellison describes such reconciliation as "visibility." [8]

Like other modern novelists, Ellison constructs his image of reality after the example of *Hamlet*, as a play within a play. The novel is both the "mirror of experience" and the "face of conscience." At the portals of the interior "theatre" stands the searcher, the philosophic "I," through whose vision the images of experience flow. The novel is thus related on simultaneous planes of narration, on the Dionysian level of felt experience, as well as on the Apollonian level of reflection—the systematic presentation of ideas. In order to examine his experience at the reflective level, Ellison constructs a kind of schematic arrangement, what Ortega y Gasset has described as "scaffold," which identifies human experience in terms of philosophical alternatives. [9]

At the first level of narration, Ellison's "I" examines much the same world as do the protagonists of Faulkner and Wright, a world divided into modes of reality called "black" and "white." But for Ellison there are shadings in this pattern; that is to say, his protagonist finds grey areas, a limited access between worlds. Indeed, some of the finest writing in this novel is given to the expression of the protagonist's emotions about his anguished movement between these modes of being. Perhaps the most dramatic point in the expressive document is that at which the protagonist's confusion about these realities reaches proportions of insanity:

WHAT IS YOUR NAME?

A tremor shook me; it was as though he had suddenly given a name to, had organized the vagueness that drifted through my head, and I was overcome with swift shame. I realized that I no longer knew my own name. I shut my eyes and shook my head with sorrow. Here was the first warm attempt to communicate with me and I was failing. I tried again, plunging into the blackness of my mind. It was no use; I found nothing but pain. . . .[10]

But Ellison's novel is more than an account of critical insanity. His protagonist is engaged in an urgent mission, for he seeks to discover in the chaotic universe in which he has his partial existence, an ethic. Ellison's protagonist may be described as Hegelian man, a symbol of humanity in search of a viable moral principle. The protagonist, the "I,"

---

[8] Ralph Ellison, *Invisible Man* (New York, 1952).

[9] See Ortega y Gasset's discussion of the contemporary search for a mode of objectification of experience in *The Dehumanization of Art: and other Writings on Art and Culture* (Garden City, New York, 1956).

[10] Ellison, *op. cit.*, p. 182.

searches for this principle externally, in the communities to which his odyssey takes him: (1) the Southern town of his birth; (2) a Negro college; (3) a segregated community in the North; (4) the Northern world of industry; (5) a revolutionary political group; (6) a Negro ghetto in a Northern city.[11] The protagonist discovers, as the absurd hero is always to discover, that there can not exist such a community; that the creation of an ethic must be, in fact, the responsibility of the individual. Thereupon, the hero takes an action described by the critic René Marill Albérès as the "descent into the self." M. Albérès has described the work of Sartre, Camus, Anouilh, and others in language appropriate to this discussion:

> Each of their heroes has for his mission to work out his destiny in solitude without the help of social patterns of divine grace, and each of these heroes also invents for his life an ethic for which the price is the refusal of all attitudes already achieved and modeled on social dishonesty and pretext.[12]

The symbol of this self-imposed alienation is for Ellison a hole in the ground, a complex image representing many things, among them what Professor Bone describes as solitude, despair, death, and the whole "underground" life of the nation.[13]

It is at this point in consciousness that a third journey takes place; indeed, has, at the beginning of the book, already taken place. For the *raison d'être* of the novel is actually this account of the third odyssey, the journey within the self. It is here that the problem left essentially unanswered by Faulkner and Wright is confronted: How can the hero find freedom in the absurd world of "black" and "white"?

Ellison's "I" examines the possibilities which commend themselves:

> I am an invisible man. . . . I am invisible, understand, simply because people refuse to see me. Like the bodiless heads you see sometimes in circus sideshows, it is as though I have been surrounded by mirrors of hard, distorting glass. When they approach me they see only my surroundings, themselves, or figments of their imagination—indeed, everything and anything except me.
>
> . . . .
>
> That invisibility to which I refer occurs because of a peculiar disposition of the eyes of those with whom I come in contact. A matter of the construction of their *inner* eyes, those eyes with which they look through their physical eyes upon reality. . . . Or again, you often doubt if you really exist. You wonder whether you aren't simply a phantom in other people's minds. Say, a figure in a nightmare which the sleeper tries

[11] See Robert Bone's discussion of Ellison, *op. cit.*, pp. 196–212.

[12] René-Marill Albérès, *La Révolte des écrivains d'aujourd'hui* (Paris: Correa, 1949), p. 15.

[13] Bone, *op. cit.*, pp. 201–03.

with all his strength to destroy. . . . You ache with the need to convince yourself that you do exist in a real world, that you're a part of all the sound and anguish and you strike out with your fists, you curse and you swear to make them recognize you. And, alas, it's seldom successful.[14]

Like Bigger, Ralph Ellison's protagonist comes to reject the vision of himself as a victim, and wills instead to assume responsibility for his own destiny:

You go along for years knowing something is wrong, then suddenly you discover that you're as transparent as air. At first you tell yourself that it's all a dirty joke, or that it's due to the "political situation." But deep down you come to suspect that you're yourself to blame, and you stand naked and shivering before the millions of eyes who look through you unseeingly.[15]

The protagonist, seeking to discern the nature of his own ethical alternatives, considers four possibilities: (1) formal segregation; (2) voluntary segregation; (3) integration; (4) revolt. Like Christmas and Bigger, Ellison's "I" chooses revolt. But the nature of his revolt is different from that of other figures whom we have considered, for it is not primarily physical. It is, rather, the revolt of consciousness—a renunciation which leads the protagonist finally into solitude. Like Dante's poet, the philosophic "I" descends into the depths of his own soul to begin the unraveling of the mystery of the self, to work out the details of his ethic. Ellison's "I" moves in paradoxical motion: backward to the beginning—the point of rebellion, the origin of his descent into despair—and, by the same token, forward in ascent to the beginning of knowledge, freedom, and visibility.

Absurd freedom for Ellison is the classic triumph of knowledge, the illumination of suffering:

Since you never recognize me even when in closest contact with me, and since, no doubt, you'll hardly believe that I exist, it won't matter if you know that I tapped a power line leading into the building and ran it into my hole in the ground. Before that I lived in the darkness into which I was chased, but now I see. I've illuminated the blackness of my invisibility—and vice versa. And so I play the invisible music of my isolation.[16]

Ellison's philosophic "I" discovers that the light which crowns torture with triumph is truth. Freedom is not escape from Hell through death or violence, but mastery of it. Like Camus' Sisyphus, Ellison's hero makes of his damnation his art. It is this qualitative heroism which

[14] Ellison, *Invisible Man*, p. 3.

[15] *Ibid*, p. 434.

[16] *Ibid*, p. 11.

gives meaning and sense to the life of the protagonist and which grants him that freedom which the absurd seeks. Ellison's final comment is a significant comment on the absurd journey: "And it is that which frightens me: Who knows but that, on the lower frequencies, I speak for you?" [17]

[17] *Ibid*, p. 439.

Two Modern Incest Heroes

by Selma Fraiberg

Freud has shown that the theme of incest in its manifold disguises is ubiquitous in the literature and art of all ages and all times. The variations upon this theme are produced by the culture and the forms and symbols which it lends to disguise, by the degree of repression which the culture dictates and by the personality of the artist who employs these materials in his work.

But until this century no writer had to contend with the idea that the universal dread of incest had its origins in a repressed wish. Freud's discovery, the unmasking of one of the great tragic themes of literature, has the effect of releasing a profound and melancholy joke from the depths of the myth. The comedy turns on the point that the object of moral dread is the object of desire, an irony that does not easily lend itself to literary treatment of incest and one that gives little scope to incest as a tragic theme. This is not to say that incest is no longer a tragic theme—it will probably endure as long as the human race— but a writer who makes use of the psychoanalytic insight in a contemporary treatment of the incest theme will find that the insight robs the work of tragic import. An Oedipus, not-knowing, who is drawn to his mother by irresistible external forces, is a tragic figure, but an Oedipus in a contemporary verison who reveals the motive of unconscious seeking of the mother has cheated us out of the vital secret, and in giving himself away his tragedy is diminished.

In this respect and others it can be argued that psychoanalysis has inhibited the modern writer to a far greater extent than it has liberated him. The insights of psychoanalysis cannot be ignored by a novelist writing today—but what is to be done with them? A clinical insight does not stir old ghosts in the psyche and bring forth unremembered feelings. On the contrary it behaves like a conjurer's trick to put down the ghosts and quiet the turbulence below. (In crude

"Two Modern Incest Heroes," by Selma Fraiberg. From Partisan Review, *XXVIII (Fall/Winter 1961), 646–961. Copyright © 1961 by* Partisan Review. *Reprinted by permission of the author and* Partisan Review.

The discussion of Thomas Mann's work which appeared in the original article has been omitted here. Ellipses indicate the omissions.

analogy with the therapeutic effects of interpretation.) If a writer wishes to produce the emotional effects of an incestuous conflict he will do much better with the conjuring tricks of his trade than those of the psychoanalyst. If he can conceal and disguise the conflict and smuggle it past the cold clinical eye of the modern reader the story may get through and surprise the unguarded regions of emotion. But if he writes a psychoanalytic version of an incestuous conflict he runs the risk of creating a clinical document.

In the case of the classic incest drama, the tension is sustained through the device of "not knowing," that is, innocence of motive. And if *Oedipus Rex* has lost none of its power over a modern audience, even one that "knows" the internal motive, it is because we have entered the dramatist's conspiracy not to know, that we accept for this moment the conventions of both the drama and another time and suspend beliefs that might interfere with enjoyment.

But a psychoanalytic version of Oedipus leaves the writer with no place to hide the motive. The play can't be written without the play-within-the-play and when the motive of unconscious seeking enters the story it has the effect of dissolving the tension. If dread, horror, and shame are the emotional concomitants of incest they are best sustained in a narrative in which the internal motive is concealed. For emotion is reinforced and heightened by the contributions of energy from unconscious sources. It is the unknown danger that raises the intensity of feeling. In the case of incest the unknown danger is the wish, and if a modern writer lays bare the unconscious motive in his narrative he will reduce the intensity of feeling. In this way the identification of motive has the same effect upon the narrative as the interpretation of a dream, i.e., when the motive is brought into consciousness the accompanying effects are diminished.

Even D. H. Lawrence could not extricate himself from this dilemma. All the fine prose and the marvelously wrought flower imagery in *Sons and Lovers* cannot overcome the clinical drabness of the mother-son love. And while Paul's later sufferings and failures in love are given complexity and texture by the device of the interlocking theme of mother-son love, once mother-love is given a strong statement in the story Lawrence cannot surprise the emotions, and the tragedy of Paul seems a little commonplace to the modern reader who has ripened on the psychological novel.

. . . There is probably some significance in the fact that two of the best incest stories I have encountered in recent years are burlesques of the incest myth. The ancient types are reassembled in gloom and foreboding to be irresistibly drawn to their destinies, but the myth fails before the modern truth; the oracle speaks false and the dream speaks true. In both the farmer's tale in Ralph Ellison's *Invisible Man* and in Thomas Mann's *The Holy Sinner*, the incest hero rises above the myth by accepting the wish as motive; the heroic act is the casting off of pretense.

. . . Ralph Ellison brings together a Negro sharecropper and a white philanthropist for the impossible meeting, the meeting which has been postponed until the white man's Judgment Day. It is the meeting that reveals the motive in the white man's abhorrence of the Negro, the black sin which is cast out in dread and loathing and rediscovered in a black brother with dread and loathing. The sin is, of course, incest, and the impossible meeting is the confrontation of the white man with his sinful motive. The meeting is envisioned by Ellison with superb wit.

Mr. Norton, the white philanthropist, appears in the early part of the novel as the distinguished visitor to the campus of a southern Negro college. The narrator, then a student, is appointed chauffeur to Mr. Norton during his visit and unwittingly steers him to the fateful meeting with the farmer, Trueblood. Mr. Norton has dedicated his life to the improvement of the Negro. His work is a monument to his dead daughter, and he speaks lyrically of her beauty, her purity and her goodness. His love for his daughter and his good works for the Negro are the two sustaining forces of his life. We do not understand yet how they are connected.

Mr. Norton has an extraordinary introduction to Mr. Trueblood, the Negro sharecropper of local fame, who has impregnated both his daughter and his wife. In fascinated horror Mr. Norton confronts the sharecropper.

"Is it true . . . I mean did you?"
"Suh?" Trueblood asked . . .
. . . "You have survived," he blurted. "But is it true . . . ?"
"*Suh?*" the farmer said, his brow wrinkling with bewilderment. . . .
. . . "You did and you are unharmed!" he shouted, his blue eyes blazing into the black face with something like envy and indignation. . . .
"You have looked upon chaos and are not destroyed!"
"No suh! I feels all right."
"You do? You feel no inner turmoil, no need to cast out the offending eye?"
"*Suh?*"
"Answer me!"
"I'm all right, suh," Trueblood said uneasily. "My eyes is all right too. And when I feels po'ly in my gut I takes a little soda and it goes away."

Trueblood is urged to tell his tale.

One night in the crowded family bed of the sharecropper's cabin Trueblood lay next to his grown daughter and found himself in a dream. It was a distorted dream of intercourse in which the dreamer finds himself in a white man's house in the bedroom of a white lady.

There follows a nightmare sequence in which the dreamer tries to escape from the embrace of the white woman and flees through the door of a grandfather clock, running with pounding heart through a hot, dark tunnel.

When the dreamer wakens he finds himself on top of his daughter in a sexual embrace. It is the moment before the climax. And here is the farmer's dilemma: If he moves to withdraw he will sin. If he stays he will sin. He cannot act without moving and he cannot move without sinning. Trueblood (urged on by his daughter) stays to sin.

Now the farmer's wife, Kate, is aroused and goes mad with horror and revulsion. Kate, posing as God's wrathful instrument, grabs an axe and brings it down upon her husband who lies hypnotized before this terrible judgment. But at the last minute he cannot bring himself to submit to the axe and turns his head to one side. The axe strikes the side of his face. Kate, ready to strike again, poises the axe and then Trueblood sees it stop, "like somebody done reached down through the roof and caught it." The axe falls behind her at this time, and Kate stumbles out the back door and vomits.

Trueblood leaves his home and, following the myth, becomes a wanderer shunned by all men. In exile he ponders his guilt. Did he sin or didn't he sin? Is a man responsible for his dreams? Trueblood does not appeal to God for a judgment, and God remains silent during Trueblood's exile. A man of a more philosophical turn of mind might have spent the rest of his life wandering in the wilderness pondering his guilt. But Trueblood is a practical man. When he finds that he cannot know his crime or his guilt, he accepts the impossibility of knowing and sees the absurdity of his exile for an unjudged crime. He decides to return to his family.

At this point Trueblood breaks with the myths. And from that moment the myth collapses, all the actors in the ancient pageant lose their lines, and the myth goes off on a lunatic rampage reversing its prophecy. Trueblood returns to his family and his sin brings him undreamed-of prosperity.

Trueblood becomes an embarrassed hero, a contemporary marvel for his white neighbors, the man who committed the blackest sin and lived to tell the tale. The white folks come to visit him and hear his story, the plain white folks who are his neighbors and educated white folks from the university who write articles about him. They pay him well for his story and take good care of him and his family. Trueblood and his pregnant daughter and his pregnant wife are perversely rewarded for sin.

The argument is subtle, here. Mr. Ellison does not consider incest a laughing matter, of course. But he understands that the inmost core of the incest myth contains a grotesque comedy, the comedy of knowing—not knowing. He has expertly brought off the bitter joke that Mr. Trueblood's dream-sin is the white man's dream-sin and that Trueblood is rewarded for offering himself as a symbol and taking the white man's sin on himself.

Ellison's tale is marvelously contrived to state the dilemma of the man of our times who can no longer hide behind the myth. He has written a kind of incest comedy in which moral dread is exposed as the other face of desire, but in this treatment he reveals an irony of such magnitude that the ancient myth acquires a new dimension as tragedy. As in the classical model the tragedy proceeds through its inevitable phases by means of the device of "not knowing," but "not knowing" in this modern incest tale is a species of self-deception, the denial of the sinful motive in the unconscious.

There are two incest heroes in Ellison's story—or one, if you like—for Mr. Trueblood is Mr. Norton's brother of the dream, his black self. Mr. Norton who listens to Mr. Trueblood's dream with dread and fascination is the witness to his own dream. Mr. Norton's dream-sin of incest is concealed from him and from the world. He atones by creating monuments to the sacred memory of his daughter, and his good works for the Negro are the symbols of his guilty partnership with the Negro: the Negro sins for Mr. Norton and Mr. Norton atones. Mr. Trueblood who sinned in a dream and wakened to find himself embracing his daughter is stripped of pretense and the protection of the myth. He is confronted with his naked self and the testimony of his dream and the act. He can still take refuge in the myth by submitting to the classical fate; for an instant he offered himself to the axe and then refused; for a short time he exiled himself but chose to come back. He became a hero because he refused to hide behind the cowardly deceptions that cloak sin; he faced the truth within himself. In this way Trueblood rose above the myth and escaped the tragic consequences. He reverses the classic fate of the incest hero. Instead of an Oedipus blinded we are given an Oedipus newly sighted.

Norton is Oedipus blinded in this story, for when he is confronted with Trueblood's dream-sin, which is his own, he refuses to see and is carried from the scene unconscious. In one of the funniest and saddest chapters of the story, the unconscious Mr. Norton is carried off to a whorehouse frequented by the Negro inmates of a local insane asylum and lies serenely unconscious in the midst of brawling and whoring while the lunatics speak unquieting truths about the white man's sickness and the black man's sickness. They are not heard, and when Norton is revived by a lucid madman (once a prominent Negro psychiatrist) everyone works quickly to put Mr. Norton together again, to shore up the fictions and pretenses, to tell him what he wants to hear and show him what he wants to see. The young Negro student who had unwittingly led Mr. Norton to the sharecropper's cabin is hastily expelled by his college for his part in bringing about the impossible meeting.

Did Mr. Trueblood sin? Mr. Ellison puts the moral problem with great delicacy and sees it in all its complexity. Is a man morally responsible for his dream? This is undoubtedly one of the most bothersome questions to emerge with Freudian psychology. Freud himself addressed himself to the problem in a little known and rarely remembered essay called "Moral Responsibility in Dreaming." Freud says "yes," and such is the confusion generated by psychoanalysis that nobody remembers that Freud himself gave cold comfort to the dream-sinners, that conscious-unconscious a man cannot escape moral responsibility; he alone is the inventor of his dream.

Trueblood, the modern incest hero, is obliged to judge his own case and cannot find the verdict. He is guilty—not-guilty in the uncertain class of modern criminals still waiting judgment with Joseph K. But he is not afflicted with their disease; he does not torment himself with unanswerable questions, and he cannot bring himself to atone for a crime that cannot be judged. There are no heroes in Joseph K.'s courtroom. K. submitted to the knife and others are consumed by their disease. But Trueblood became a hero because he refused the refuge of mind-sickness, and his manhood refused the axe. He did not bargain with God in the wilderness, but fairly judged his own worthiness to live and manfully returned to his living.

Now of course Ellison is not writing a case for incest. Mr. Trueblood's prosperity is a bitter joke, and to understand the joke in all its complexity we need to study the conduct of God, Himself, during this case. For it strikes us that God showed a considerable disregard for the conventions of the incest tale. His judgment appears to be far more lenient than that of Trueblood's human judges. He stayed the hand of Kate Trueblood when she brought the axe down the second time and was satisfied that the sinner should bear his judgment in the unhealing sore, the mark of the axe's first blow. When Kate, posing as God's wrathful instrument, demanded the sacrifice of Trueblood's manhood, God gave no sign when the axe descended for its first blow and seemed to wait for the sign from Trueblood. Trueblood's instinctive turning aside was the affirmation of his manhood, and God, approving, stayed the hand of Kate when she was about to bring the axe down for the second blow.

When Trueblood goes forth into the wilderness we are given no sign as to God's intentions. The myth supports the interpretation that God looks favorably upon wandering in the wilderness for crimes of various classes, but when Trueblood decides to go home and face his crime and assume his masculine prerogatives, God approves and rewards him by causing him to prosper. This suggests to me that God is sick of naked and sightless fools wandering in the wilderness and that any man who wants to go home and face up to things may get His blessings.

The Rebirth of the Artist

by Ellin Horowitz

Welcome O Life! I go to encounter for the millionth time the reality of experience and to forge in the smithy of my soul the uncreated conscience of my race.

James Joyce, *A Portrait of the Artist as a Young Man*

Invisible Man is another kind of portrait of the artist, the making of an exile. Ralph Ellison's book, like Joyce's, takes its hero through a series of initiatory episodes from which he emerges a new man, an individual with the god-like power to create. . . .

A profitable method of dealing with *Invisible Man* is to see the action as a series of initiations in which the hero passes through several stages and groups of identification. The changes of identity are accompanied by somewhat formal rituals resembling the primitive's rites of passage. The primitive recognizes that man changes his identity as he passes from one stage or group to another and accompanies this transition by rituals that are essentially symbolic representations of birth, purification and regeneration in nature.

Ellison's narrative is a series of such initiatory experiences set within a cyclical framework of the mystic initiation of the artist. The rites of passage take the hero through several stages in which he acts out his various and conflicting sub-personalities. When he has won his freedom he is reborn as the artist, the only actor in our society whose "end" is a search beneath the label for what is individual.

The narrator begins his story in the pit and in a flashback takes his hero through the experience that led up to his descent. Finally, in the epilogue, there is a union between the innocent hero and the

"The Rebirth of the Artist" by Ellin Horowitz, from On Contemporary Literature, *ed. Richard Kostelanetz (New York: Avon Books, 1964), pp. 330–46. Copyright © 1964 The Hearst Corporation. Reprinted by permission of the publisher. Passages on sources and images more fully discussed elsewhere in this volume have been omitted.*

artist who has achieved wisdom; the central duality lies in that juxtaposition between the two I's. The element of confession in the first person narration of *Invisible Man* suggests its function as a cathartic. The artist tells us his story from the pit so that he may rise at the end.

The hero begins his career in a Southern town as a docile innocent who dreams of becoming educated and pleasing the white community. The narrative is the story of his expulsion from this Eden of illusion.

The first uneasy note in the hero's youthful paradise is the recurring voice of his grandfather who on his deathbed told the boy that he had been a spy all his life. "I want you to overcome 'em with yesses, undermine 'em with grins, agree 'em to death and destruction, let 'em swaller you 'till they vomit or bust wide open." Though the meekest of men he had spoken of his meekness as something dangerous. This is essentially the ancient Chinese strategy of absorbing the conqueror in order to keep one's own identity. When things go well for the hero he feels guilty, as though he were unconsciously obeying his grandfather's advice. For conduct defined as treachery he is praised by the most "lily-white" men of the town (i.e., "that's pretty white of you"). Throughout the hero is fearful of upsetting white domination, and the meaning of his grandfather's sphinx-like riddle becomes a key problem ("The old man's words were like a curse").

The smoker scene is the crucial initiatory experience of the hero's boyhood. His art will be born out of blood, chaos, and humiliation—the conditions under which he gives his first speech on The Virtue of Humility. At the height of a battle-royal he sees the prostitute who taunts him as a bird girl, and, as in Joyce, this is the moment the hero's art is born. He will suffer anything in order to give his speech. Ironically, the only prophecy born out of the dark bloody arena is a speech on humility, and the reward, a scholarship, is the key to the world of Negro yes-sayers and repressed respectability. It is the first item in the prize briefcase the hero will always carry. He is told: "Keep developing as you are and someday it will be filled with important papers that will help you shape the destiny of your people." The irony is pointed at the articles he will later carry in the briefcase, which is equated throughout with the hero's unconscious; he will continue collecting things in it, the things he wishes to put away, the symbols of his disillusionment. It becomes a record of his being and his "badge of office" like the Shamen's magic bag.

At the second stage the hero is seen at college aspiring to be an educator and identifying with the college president Bledsoe (long suffering bled-so). Bledsoe is one of various types of Negroes pictured here as tempters; others are a Booker T. Washington Negro, the Uncle Tom educator, the kind who "keeps his place," the semi-mythic Founder, and blind Barbee who says "see ahead." Bledsoe himself is the seemingly unctuous servant who is in truth deadly aggressive. Despite power, prestige, white friends, and Cadillacs he somehow arranges his pants so they will sag at the knees and his feet shuffle to suggest a past on a chain gang. Like the hero's grandfather he says, I seem obsequious but really rule them all. For power he will say yes and aid white men in subjugating his people. The hero's grandfather, however, made no claim to rule. He simply allowed himself to be swallowed so that the white man would choke.

The fall from the college paradise occurs when the hero inadvertently shows a Northern trustee do-gooder the seamier side of Negro life outside the Utopian college grounds. The seamy side appears in the countryside's most notorious Negro, a kind of monster described by progressive Negroes with disgust as "field niggerism." The scene itself is a monstrous parody of Southern genre writing about Negroes, highlighted by an Erskine Caldwell account of the Negro's incestuous relations with his daughter. Not so strangely, minorities seem to be traditionally characterized as oversexed and immoral, and here the image of the Negro as an uncivilized instinctive animal and "big black rapist" is clearly the transference of the forbidden on to the scapegoat people. The trustee, Norton (perhaps a nasty pun on Charles Eliot Norton, as the other Northerner is called Emerson), listens with a voyeur's perverse fascination because he has had just these desires towards his own daughter, and he concludes by paying the old Negro for doing it for him.

For this crime, the acceptance of reality and an unconscious revolt against yesing the white man, the hero is expelled from grace and must leave the sanctuary of school. "Here with the quiet greenness I possessed the only identity I had ever known and I was losing it."

The great exodus following the expulsion is a transition from the South to Harlem. Travel itself suggests a symbolic change of identity but in these first days in the North he continues to pattern himself on the old college ideal. Despite the escape by geography he remains invisible in Harlem's black against black. Dreaming of a great future he remembers always to deodorize so "they" won't think "all of us smell bad," and to be on time, "not any c.p. (colored people) time." He rejects pork chops and grits for bacon and eggs, but hearing an ashman's song begins to "go back to things I had long ago shut out of my mind."

The letter of introduction which was to bring him success proves to be the letter his grandfather showed him in a dream—the letter that says, in essence, "keep this nigger boy running." Kenneth Burke speaks of this advice as a Belerophontic letter, the message the character carries that contains his fate. Now the innocent first sees himself as deceived and betrayed. This is exactly what will happen to him; they all keep this "nigger" running. Everyone, white and black, seems in a conspiracy to keep him on the inexorable journey towards a self.

The following factory scene is a wild vision of the position of the Negro in a black-white world. Seeing the building at a distance "was like watching some vast patriotic ceremony." Flags flutter around a great white sign bearing the company slogan: "Keep America pure with Liberty Paints." The factory's chief patriotic contribution is their color "optic white," related to the dominant theme of sight and blindness, visibility and invisibility, white and black. The hero's job is to make white paint by putting a drop of seemingly magic solution into a can of black liquid, but he cannot seem to make it white enough and when it is white he sees only grey (recalling the white campus and the dim Negro cabins nearby).

Again the Negro appears as the victim, the result of the conscious or unconscious torture of one man to another. The hero remains unseen to those about him who see only what they need or want to see. To the unions he is a company fink, while to Lucius Brockway he is an educated Negro who doesn't know his place and probably belongs to the union. Each uses him for his own ends. Lucius, the old Negro who tends the furnace, says he is the one who really makes the paint white; "I dips my finger in and sweets it." This black finger and the black liquid are needed to make the paint white. It is the Negro who keeps America pure by acting as the scapegoat for all sins (a deliberately grim joke for purity is identified with whiteness).

Lucius Brockway is the Negro who maintains his invisibility, going underground (he works in the basement), and worshipping the boss and white supremacy. He created the company slogan: "If it's optic white it's the right white," reminiscent of the folk song's refrain, "If you're white you're right, but if you're black, get back, get back, get back."

The hero's first act of revolt is his unconscious inability to make white paint, for implicit in his failure is the overthrow of Lucius Brockway, one of the dominant authority images. The act of rebellion culminates in a furnace explosion with its images of the inferno, and a loss of consciousness which functions as the ritualistic-death of the initiate.

The scene that follows in the factory hospital is clearly a strange vision of birth with suggestions of lobotomy and castration. The hero lies in a womb-like box as figures in white perform a macabre operation intending to turn him into a "vegetable." During the mock shock therapy he appears as a ludicrous dancing minstrel darky, the harmless silly fellow the white world would like to believe in to allay their fears. Recovering consciousness he feels his limbs amputated; he is like a child, without a past, helpless, and lost in a "vast whiteness." The "delivery" is complete with the literal cutting of an umbilical cord. The old personality is dead and the initiate has a new identity born out of the machine. Because he has lost his past he is considered cured but when questioned about Buckeye the Rabbit he remembers playing this part as a child and is brought back through reversion to the folk tradition of which he is an unacknowledged part: "I could no more escape than I could think of my own identity. Perhaps, I thought, the two things are involved with each other. When I discover who I am I'll be free."

Man is never a constant unified being. Always in a state of transition, he is not one but many multiple subidentities. Thus duality is essential in the notion of rebirth. The hero, caught in the conflict between old and new, is described in terms of a disassociated personality: "I had the feeling that I had . . . used words and expressed attitudes not my own, that I was in the grip of some alien personality lodged deep within me." The schizophrenic behavior of the tribal shamen is thought to indicate possession by the gods and Ellison's hero displays some of the symptoms of the mad prophet. Later, before his first speech for the Brotherhood he describes his ambivalence:

> This was a new phase, I realized, a new beginning, and I would have to take that part of myself that looked on with remote eyes and keep it always at the distance of the campus. . . . Perhaps that part of me, that observed listlessly but saw all, was still the urging part, the dissenting voice—the traitor self that always threatened internal discord.

Throughout the narrative the hero stands between submission and rebellion like a tragic hero torn between two conflicting necessities. In order to achieve the new life of the ritual, the god, in Freud's terms the father, must be slain. The guilty answering voice demands submission, for parricide is the greatest of man's crimes. The hero's traitor voice is the voice of the rebellious son. A dream in the prologue re-creates the Freudian myth of the primal horde in racial terms. Here a Negro woman poisons her white master-husband to save him from a more brutal sacrifice by their white-hating sons. She tells the hero that she loved her husband but she loved freedom more. While she cries her sons laugh and the hero observes: "I too have become acquainted with ambivalence."

The alternate strategies offered the Negro, to submit or to rebel, reflect the traditional ambivalence of the son. The notion of the great white father and the simple Negro children who must be protected by the parental taboos of white supremacy would suggest that the entire racial division can be seen in terms of the relationship between father and son. The white man's advice to the Negro to "keep his place" is the father's advice and the threat in both cases is sexual. In *Invisible Man* the authoritarian figures consistently play the role of subjugating the hero, punishing him for the crime of asserting his identity, seen as the son's rebellion. The displaced guilt running throughout the narrative can be traced to the desire to overthrow the father and is certainly linked with the dominant castration imagery. Throughout, the hero identifies with authority figures, torn between submission and rebellion, feeling like a criminal but not knowing why he is guilty. . . . .

It should be made clear that the father-god figures in the narrative are not always white men although white seems to function generally as the image rebelled against. Actually almost every major character in the novel is a variation on this theme. The college Founder, described as part Horatio Alger, part Christ, is called a "cold father symbol" and the narrator derives great pleasure from seeing pigeons soil his statue. Norton is "a god, a force," a "messiah" and a "great white father." Later Brother Jack is called a "great white father" who, for all his seeming liberalism, should really be called "Marse Jack" as he is the field boss in a white supremacy state. He watches his underlings "like a bemused father listening to the performance of his adoring children," and is later compared, in a quite Freudian sense, with a bulldog the hero feared as a child. Finally, at the conclusion, Ras appears as an angry black god wreaking destruction.

After the factory explosion the hero begins a new life mothered by Mary. Not so curiously his family, like Christ's, is fatherless. Mary is a reminder of his past, stable and comforting, but she demands some notable achievement that will benefit the race. As Mary's son he must seek his appointed role. Now he can accept his true identity symbolized in the acceptance of Negro food. He eats yams boldly on the street; "They're my birthmark . . . I yam what I am." This realization, in turn, enables him to deliver the eviction speech (in echo of Antony's address to the Romans) that wins him a position in the Brotherhood. . . .

With the entrance into the Brotherhood comes another transformation. The change in group identification is symbolized by a new set of clothes, a new name, and a new family. (With the concept of maternity conferring rebirth all initiates become brothers.) Despite his new family and role the hero cannot rid himself of a broken bank, the grinning comic Negro image he carries in his briefcase. Brother Jack too speaks of the sacrifice of the old self for new life: "You have not completely shed that old agrarian self, but it's dead and you will throw it off and emerge with something new."

The first speech for the Brotherhood is delivered in an arena reminiscent of the earlier smoker scene. The hero feels curiously unsure of his identity, fearing he will forget his new name, or be recognized. It is a feeling of schizoid disassociation; the hero is seen as the possessed prophet whose magic lies in his speeches and his power to convert. The entire narrative, in fact, is later described as his "raving." . . .

In the concluding chapters the hero stands between the opposing forces of the Brotherhood and Ras the Exhorter, the Negro nationalist leader; both sides see him as a traitor. To escape his only recourse is the ultimate invisibility and his initial move in this last transformation is the disguise of dark glasses in which he can neither see nor be seen. Speaking to a friend he had the feeling "that the old man before me was not Brother Macao at all, but someone else disguised to confuse me." The glasses here function as the blindness of Oedipus.

In the large hat and uniform of a zoot suiter, he no longer has any identity. "It was as though by dressing and walking a certain way, I had enlisted in a fraternity in which I was recognized at a glance— not by features, but by clothes, uniform, by gait."

The key to the novel then is not actually invisibility. In the new disguise "I'd be seen in a snowstorm but they'd think I was someone else." He can be seen but not in his own identity because he is constantly changing. The metaphysical center of the novel is Rinehart for whom the hero is mistaken. Rinehart is a chameleon: confidence man, runner, gambler, briber, lover, and Reverend. Could he himself be both rind and hart? The hero seizes upon this possibility of invisibility through multiple personality. He had never seen the notorious Rinehart who is not invisible but many things, the charlatan-Reverend who advertises, "Let there be light," and "Behold the seen unseen." Perhaps only this man of many possibilities is at home in a world without boundaries where no one is anyone. Freedom, he discovers, is not only the recognition of necessity, it is the recognition of possibility. "I was and yet I was invisible, that was the fundamental contradiction. I was and yet I was unseen . . . I sensed another frightening world of possibilities. For now I could agree with Brother Jack without agreeing." Now he understands how to follow his grandfather's advice. This "choke 'em with yesses" strategy is metaphorically the going underground.

The action concludes with a vast apocalyptic image of the end of the world and the destruction of an angry god. The riot grows out of the Party's sacrifice of Harlem and the death of Tod Clifton avenged by Ras in the costume of an Abyssinian chieftain. The hero, caught between the opposing forces, runs through streets flooded with water (anticipating a new creation) as he tries to return to the mother Mary. His glasses are broken and he still carries his briefcase.

The running ceases only when he is driven into the pit—a coal cellar, for a Negro in a coal cellar is invisible. This is the dark womb which will be the source of new life just as the black coal cellar is the source of heat and light. To light his way out of the pit he must literally and symbolically burn the contents of his briefcase—the threatening letter written by Brother Jack, his Brotherhood name and identity, the scholarship, the letter that kept him running, Mary's bank, and the dancing doll, Brother Tarp's chain gang link which he received instead of his grandfather's watch as a son's legacy, the Party pamphlets, and Rinehart's promise to "Behold the seen unseen."

In his dream, Norton, Bledsoe, and Emerson return to demand his submission and castrate him for this final rebellion. The castration acts as the ultimate dispelling of illusions whereby the hero gains the right to see. Like the Fisher King his impotence seems a prerequisite for his life-giving role. Here, as in ancient ritual, the powers of reproduction are sacrificed and scattered on the water for ever-renewing life.

The hero can no longer return to Mary (because he is castrated), or to his old life (because he has no illusions). In the meantime he will remain underground. "The end was in the beginning." . . .

. . . Through his hero's varied roles the author has acted out the opposing strategies offered the Negro, of being "for" society or "against" it. The new vision born out of the hero's conflict seems to be an attitude of comic ambivalence that allows him to embrace the complexity. Within the paradox of acceptance-rejection the world becomes one of infinite possibility. Thus the hero is neither white nor black but invisible in a world which is neither good nor evil but good-and-evil. "So it is that now I denounce and defend, or feel prepared to defend. I condemn and affirm, say no and say yes, say yes and say no." Ellison's hero is not reborn in traditional triumph. He will emerge with a realistic acceptance of the limitations of society (". . . for all life seen from the hole of invisibility is absurd"), and his own role (". . . and humanity is won by continuing to play in face of certain defeat").

The curious note in this almost neat equation is the stronger emphasis given the sense of limitation and doubt. The narrator's view often appears to have less of the positive quality of union than the tentative quality of hedging. Ellison seems strangely divided about his theme and the sense of hesitancy and confusion in the epilogue would seem to deny the affirmation to be gained by a descent into darkness. The hero has not come very far beyond his initial understanding of invisibility, a fine but limited notion. He has become a prophet but does not have much to prophesy. While the author need not offer us glory and salvation, the structure of the narrative does suggest a rebirth in proportion to the intensity and conviction of the fearsome descent. Ellison's hero, it seems, will emerge simply because he has no real choice and the epilogue, his prophecy, is certainly the least effective piece of writing in the novel. We feel that the author searches for something positive but seems undercut by doubt; significantly, almost all of the writing in the epilogue is qualified or framed as questions. The conclusion is haunted by a curious sense of fear that would deny affirmation and one cannot help but associate this with the castration fear which undercuts all the hero's attempts at rebellion.

Ellison has made poetry out of being invisible by putting it down in black and white, and the hero's failure to find affirmation in his darkness is recompensed by the savage and enlightened vision of that darkness. Ralph Ellison has written an extremely important novel, one that goes far beyond social protest though it is a protest and could scarcely help but be. Ellison neither rises above nor renounces his identity as a Negro, but uses it as the key to an understanding of the meaning and experience of alienation and isolation. His conflict belongs to all of us. It is externalized in the very real division of our society into white and black; white does not see black and this is all our fates. Having descended into such darkness Ellison has gained the right, the insight, and the responsibility to prophecy. The narrator concludes: "Who knows but that, on the lower frequencies, I speak for you?"

The Image of Man as Portrayed by
Ralph Ellison

by Therman B. O'Daniel

In 1952, Ralph Ellison published his first and only novel, *Invisible Man*. Immediately, the critics rather generally acclaimed it to be an important book, and a significant achievement. One critic hailed it as, "the most impressive work of fiction by an American Negro which I have ever read . . .";[1] while two others considered it to be "an exceptionally good book . . .";[2] and "a resolutely honest, tormented, profoundly American book . . .";[3] and still another was moved to state that—"the language of literary criticism seems shallow and patronizing when one has to speak of a book like this." [4] On the basis of the high critical approval, of which these statements are samples, *Invisible Man* proceeded to win the National Book Award as the best American novel of that year.

Since then, articles upon articles on Ellison's novel have appeared in the scholarly journals, in general magazines, and in books; until, at the present time, the body of critical literature on the work and its author is tremendous.

Several things, perhaps, may account for the unusual amount of attention which Ellison's book has received. First of all, it is actually a remarkably good book, an interesting and exciting work of fiction which, beginning with the Prologue, immediately catches the reader's attention and holds on to it tenaciously as the story unfolds. Secondly, it is a complicated and highly involved novel which employs a combination of several techniques—realism, impressionism, and surrealism.

"The Image of Man as Portrayed by Ralph Ellison" by Therman B. O'Daniel. From CLA Journal, X *(June 1967), 277–84. Copyright © 1967 by College Language Association. Reprinted by permission of the author and the College Language Association.*

[1] Orville Prescott, *The New York Times* (April 16, 1952), p. 25.

[2] Anthony West, "Ralph Ellison," *Principles and Persuasions* (New York, 1957), p. 212. [See this volume, pp. 102–6—Ed.]

[3] Wright Morris, *New York Times Book Review* (April 13, 1952), p. 5.

[4] Delmore Schwartz, *Partisan Review*, XIX (May–June 1952), p. 359.

And being a creative work of this type, it is sprinkled throughout with dreams and symbols—some resolved and some unresolved—and nothing pleases the modern critic more than to come upon a work like this in which he can sink his interpretive teeth and gnaw away at possible solutions.

One critic, for instance, considers Trueblood, Ellison's peasant farmer who has an incestuous relationship with his daughter, to be a modern incest hero, "a man who rises above the myth by acknowledging the unconscious motive." By refusing "the refuge of the myth, the refuge of *not knowing,* and by undeceiving [himself he reverses] the prophecy. We are left to conclude that it is the myth that destroys and that the heroic act for modern man is the casting off of pretense." [5]

Another critic, in the September (1966) Issue of the *Walt Whitman Review* has found in Homer A. Barbee's eulogy to the Founder and First President of Ellison's unnamed Southern Negro college, all of the symbols of Walt Whitman's "When Lilacs Last in the Dooryard Bloom'd."

> All the Whitman symbols [he writes] are there: the lilac, the star, and the thrush—the bells and the funeral train—but, and I do not think that this point can be emphasized too heavily, Ellison employs them for almost entirely opposite reasons than did the bard of American poetry. I feel such a critic as Charles Feidelson, Jr. to be correct when he concludes that Whitman was attempting in his poem to measure the potential of the poetic mind within the framework of the death of the great emancipator, Abraham Lincoln. But Ellison is much less concerned with poetic potential than with more pessimistic ideas, for the reader is quick to recognize that he uses these same symbols of the lilac, star, and thrush to measure the great irony and bitter disillusion of racial betrayal brought about after the death of another great fighter for emancipation, the beloved Founder—Ellison's picture of a black and mythical Lincoln.[6]

These few illustrations partially indicate the kind of modern allegorical and symbolical novel *Invisible Man* is, but it is more—much more. Basically, Ellison's book is an extended, complicated piece of plotted prose fiction designed, like most novels, to present as vividly as possible the image of its protagonist, or main character. In Ellison's case, the main character in his novel is a male American—specifically, an American Negro man. Now, in order to make his image as full and as rounded as possible, the author pulls out, as it were, all of the stops on his mighty fictional organ, permitting all of the pipes to blast out their eclectic sounds upon the American scene.

[5] Selma Fraiberg, "Two Modern Incest Heroes," *Partisan Review,* XXVIII, 5–6 (1961), pp. 660–61. [See this volume, pp. 73–79—ED.]

[6] Marvin E. Mengeling, "Whitman and Ellison: Older Symbols in a Modern Mainstream," *Walt Whitman Review,* XII (September 1966), p. 68.

Hence, *Invisible Man* is many things in one. It has been described as a modern picaresque novel, owing some debt to Mark Twain.[7] Readers acquainted with Melville's works might be quick to notice some parts of Ellison's book which remind them, in a peculiar way, of *The Confidence Man*. On the other hand, *Invisible Man* is certainly a devastating satire after the manner—in its own distinctive way, of course—of the eighteenth century English tradition, and it is as bitter in parts—but certainly not throughout—as Swift's *Gulliver's Travels*, but with the satire being handled in a cleverly deceptive, indirect manner in order to lessen the harshness of its impact. Then too, possessing both prologue and epilogue, Ellison's work suggests its structural kinship with the classical drama; and opening at the point in the protagonist's life, when he has just completed high school—*in medias res*, so to speak—a young black Ulysses about to be launched on his American odyssey—the novel is seen to possess much of the machinery of an epic in prose. In addition, there is its educational content, the treatment of which links it with the educational novel—but again, in a peculiarly modern and American way.

But there have been many novels in which an American Negro protagonist has been vividly portrayed, and many of these have been written by Negro authors. In what way, then, is Ellison's book different?

The answer to this question partly lies, I think, in what the very perceptive critic the late Alain Locke said about the book some years ago, soon after it was published. After stating that: "Ralph Ellison is a protégé of Wright, who predicted for him a bright literary future"; and after criticizing Ellison for some blemishes found in his work, namely his "verbosity and [excessive use of] hyperbole," he said that *Invisible Man* was "written in a style of great force and originality," and that the novel represented "both in style and conception a new height of literary achievement." Then continuing at some further length, he added:

The life story of its hero, obviously semi-autobiographic, ranges from the typical South of a few years back to the metropolitan North of New York and vicinity. Conceptually it runs also almost the whole gamut of class in American society and is interracial at all stages, even in the deep South from the benefactor patron of the college visiting for Founders Day to the sinister "crackers" of the rural backwoods. It is in fact one of the best integrated accounts of interaction between whites and Negroes in American society that has yet been presented, with all characters portrayed in the same balance and perspective. Ellison's philosophy of characterization, incisive, realistic, unsparing of physical and psychological detail—all his major characters are stripped bare to the skin

[7] Robert A. Bone, "Ralph Ellison and the Uses of Imagination," *Anger, and Beyond*, ed. Herbert Hill (New York, 1966), p. 94. [See this volume, pp. 22-31—ED.]

and bone, so to speak—is close to the best European realism in that it
is so three-dimensional. We see a grand caravan of types, all registered
first person on the sensitive but rather cynical retina of the young Negro
protagonist. In the South, the patronizing but well-intentioned school
trustee, the piously hypocritical Negro school principal, the gauche,
naive but not too honest students, the disillusioned, institutionalized war
veterans, the townsfolk, the peasants of the countryside, white and black,
and most particularly the unforgettable earthy peasant character of Jim
Trueblood. In the North, the pageant resumes with all sorts and manner of men and women: the financiers of Wall Street and their deca-
dent jazz-loving sons, factory workers, pro and anti-union varieties,
the urban peasants and their homely oddities, parlor-pinks and hard
inner-core communists, race leaders, educated and illiterate, each after
his kind—and the Harlem community generally displayed finally at
frenetic tension in its one big authentic riot. Stylistically all this unrolls
in a volcanic flow of vivid, sometimes livid imagery, a tour de force of
psychological realism. A double symbolic meaning piled on top of this
realism gives the book its distinctive and most original tone and flavor:
Invisible Man is actually a surrealistic novel because of this, and but for
its lack of restraint would rank among the very best of the genre. But
the unrestrained bravado of treatment, riding loose rein at full gallop
most of the time and the overprecious bravura of phrase and diction
weight it down where otherwise it would soar in well-controlled virtu-
osity. Many readers will be shocked at Ellison's daring franknesses and
dazed by his emotional intensity but these are an integral part of the
book's great merit. For once, too, here is a Negro writer capable of real
and sustained irony.[8]

The fact that Ellison, as Locke points out, is a "writer capable of
real and sustained irony," is another reason why *Invisible Man* is an
unusually distinctive novel. Considering the fact that the American
Negro has been subjected to two major types of prejudice—racial
prejudice and color prejudice—the mere title of this work is pregnant
with ironic implications. What it ironically implies is that the Negro,
whose color can be seen from afar, and whose blackness is often directly
the cause of his being subjected to the most humiliating experiences,
cannot be seen at all because he is *invisible!*

And when we remember what the narrator, who is the Invisible
Man of the story, has told us in the very first paragraph of the Prologue, namely, that he is really not invisible at all; that he is "a man
of substance, of flesh and bone, fiber and liquids"—and that he "might
even be said to possess a mind"; and when we remember his telling us:
"I am invisible, understand, simply because people refuse to see
me. . . . When they approach me they see only my surroundings,
themselves, or figments of their imagination—indeed, everything and

[8] Alain Locke, "From *Native Son* to *Invisible Man:* A Review of the Literature
of the Negro for 1952," *Phylon*, XIV (First Quarter 1953), pp. 34–35.

anything except me"; the irony instead of decreasing mounts a hundredfold. For what more humiliating experience is there for a man to have than to be ignored.

Critic Locke mentioned two other things in his excellent analysis of *Invisible Man* which its author, Ralph Ellison, has gone to some lengths to deny. Locke stated that the life story of the novel's hero was "obviously semi-autobiographic," and taking all things into consideration, including the critic's use of the prefix *semi* which stresses the fact that he meant that the author made imaginative use—and not necessarily literal use—of some autobiographical facts, this would seem to be a reasonably sound assertion to make.

Author Ellison's statement on this point, however, is an emphatic no. In an interview on "The Art of Fiction" with Alfred Chester and Vilma Howard, his very first statement is the following: "Let me say right now that my book [*Invisible Man*] is not an autogiobraphical work." [9]

Except for a curious interest in the truth, whether this answer or another had been given on this particular point is relatively unimportant as far as the artistry of the novel is concerned. But Locke's other statement: "Ralph Ellison is a protégé of Wright," because it is much more pertinent, might engage our attention for a moment, and lead to the conclusion of this brief discussion.

Ellison was an admirer of Richard Wright; was encouraged by Wright to study and learn the technique of the literary craft; and had his first piece of writing, a book review, published in Wright's magazine, *New Challenge;* but, in several of the essays in *Shadow and Act,* he denied that his relationship to Wright was ever that of a protégé.

Here again, the interested and careful reader might wonder whether Ellison did not consciously learn more from Wright than he cares to admit; or whether, unconsciously, he did not learn more from him than he realized. One thing is certain, both Baldwin and Ellison—though Ellison, not quite to the unreasonable extent as Baldwin—go to a considerable amount of unnecessary trouble to set very restricted limitations upon their debt to the author of *Native Son* and *Black Boy.*

On the other hand, it is true that Wright and Ellison—though both Negroes—are products of different backgrounds. Wright's early experiences were unforgettably bitter, and he possessed the talent—unaided by hardly any formal education—to describe them in prose that is so realistically vivid and powerful that it is sometimes frightening and painful to read. Ellison, although his family was poor, is from the Negro middle class. He was educated in a fairly good high school where the fine arts were taught; studied music formally and later became a professional musician; knew about symphonies and wanted to write one; had three years of college study; knew about sculpture and wanted to be a sculptor; and, as a matter of fact, he knew what being a Renaissance Man meant, and wanted to be one of those too. He came to think seriously of writing last, and when he was encouraged by Richard Wright, he wanted to be a writer also. But, as we have said, the backgrounds of the two men were decidedly different. Wherein Ellison might delight in having learned from Hemingway the sportsmanly art of "wing-shooting," [10] Black Boy Wright, no doubt, must often have come dangerously close to being shot.

"And yet, from the very beginning," states Ellison, when he seriously considered becoming a writer, "I wanted to write about American Negro experience and I suspected that what was important, what made the difference lay in the perspective from which it was viewed." [11]

It is this difference between the two men—a difference in their backgrounds which led to a difference in the perspective from which each viewed American Negro life—that makes their writings different. Richard Wright's experiences as an American Negro caused him to write tragedies; Ralph Ellison's experiences, which he readily admits were never "too uncomfortable," [12] caused him to write in his *Invisible Man,* a tragicomedy. In several of its parts, *Invisible Man* is a bitterly, ironic, tragic book, but like all tragicomedies it has an incongruously happy ending.

Richard Wright's Black Boy possessed no powers of legerdemain which enabled him to disguise himself at will, as Ellison's Rinehart, or to become, at other times, completely invisible. For him there was no hiding place in a symbolic subterranean coal bin. He had to face up to the cruel and excruciatingly brutal forces of reality.

But Ralph Ellison, who presents a different image of man in his *Invisible Man,* continues to insist that:

> For better or worse, whatever there is of value in Negro life is an American heritage and as such it must be preserved. Besides, I am unwilling to see those values which I would celebrate in fiction as existing sheerly through terror; they are a result of a tragicomic confrontation of life.[13]

It is then, this attitude, this philosophy of life, that enabled Ellison to portray in his novel, perhaps the best balanced and most complete and comprehensive image of the American Negro that has yet been presented by any contemporary writer. Some realism, some pessimism, a considerable amount of disillusionment, some bitter irony and satire, and even some hate are all found in this unusual novel. But since Ellison is definitely a romanticist and an optimist, some humor, some

[10] *Ibid.,* p. 168.
[11] *Ibid.,* p. 16.
[12] *Ibid.,* p. 142.
[13] *Ibid.,* p. 22.

hope, and some love are also found in it. In the final pages of the Epilogue of *Invisible Man* he writes: "I have been hurt to the point of abysmal pain, hurt to the point of invisibility. And I defend because in spite of all I find that I love. In order to get some of it down I *have* to love. I sell you no phony forgiveness, I'm a desperate man— but too much of your life will be lost, its meaning lost, unless you approach it as much through love as through hate." [14]

[14] Ralph Ellison, *Invisible Man* (New York, 1952), pp. 437–38.

PART TWO

View Points

Lloyd L. Brown: The Deep Pit

"Whence all this passion toward conformity?" asks Ralph Ellison at the end of his novel, *Invisible Man*. He should know, because his whole book conforms exactly to the formula for literary success in today's market. Despite the murkiness of his *avant-garde* symbolism, the pattern is clear and may be charted as precisely as a publisher's quarterly sales report.

Chapter 1: A 12-page scene of *sadism* (a command performance of 10 Negro youths savagely beating each other for the Bourbons' reward of scattered coins), *sex* (a dance by a naked whore with a "small American flag tattooed upon her belly"), and *shock* (literally applied to the performers by an electrically charged rug).

Chapter 2: Featuring a 14-page scene in which a poor Negro farmer tells a white millionaire in great detail how he committed incest with his daughter; and the millionaire, who burns to do the same to his own daughter, rewards the narrator with a hundred-dollar bill.

And so on, to the central design of American Century literature—anti–Communism.

Author Ellison will reap more than scattered change or a crumpled bill for *his* performance. *Invisible Man* is already visible on the best-seller lists. The quivering excitement of the commercial reviewers matches that of the panting millionaire.

Strangely, there is much truth in their shouts of acclaim: "It is a sensational and feverishly emotional book. It will shock and sicken some readers . . . the hero is a symbol of doubt, perplexity, betrayal and defeat . . . tough, brutal and [again] sensational," says Orville Prescott in the New York *Times* about "the most impressive work of fiction by an American Negro which I have ever read."

"Here," writes Daniel James in the war-mongering *New Leader,* "the author establishes, in new terms, the commonness of every human's fate: nothingness."

"Authentic air of unreality," exults the reviewer in the Sunday

"The Deep Pit" by Lloyd L. Brown. From Masses & Mainstream, *V (June 1952), 62–64. Copyright © 1952 by* Masses & Mainstream. *Reprinted by permission of the author.*

Times, about the part dealing with the "Brotherhood" (Ellison's euphemism for the Communist Party).

The Sunday New York *Herald Tribune* man knows what he likes too:

> "For a grand finale there's the hot, dry August night of the big riot when the hungry looted, when Ras the destroyer—of white appeasers— alone was out for blood; when Sybil, the chestnut-haired nymphomaniac, was raped by Santa Claus, and when the Invisible Man, still clutching his briefcase, fell through an open grill into a coal cellar—and stayed there to write a book. . . ."

The *Saturday Review of Literature* is also impressed with this work that is as " 'unreal' as a surrealist painting. . . . It is unlikely that *Invisible Man* is intended to be a realistic novel although the detail is as real as the peeling paint on an old house."

At this point a reviewer in *M&M* might very well say "Amen!" and leave the unpleasant subject. But the commercial claque does more than extol Ellison's "surrealist horror," "well-ordered dissonance," "Dostoyevskianism," and thrill to "Harlem's slough of despond." We see that the same *Saturday Review* critic who is happily certain that this is not a realistic novel insists that ". . . *here, for the first time, is the whole truth about the Negro in America.*"

The mind reels before a statement such as that, compounded as it is of an ignorance so stupendous that it can only be matched by its arrogance.

Ostensibly set in Negro life, the novel is profoundly anti-Negro and it is this quality which moved several of the chauvinist critics to say that its author has "transcended race" and "writes as well as a white man"—the highest accolade they can bestow!

Here, as in James Jones' whine *From Here to Eternity,* is the one-man-against-the-world theme, a theme which cannot tell the "whole truth" or any part of the truth about the Negro people in America or about any other people anywhere.

Ellison's narrator-hero is a shadowy concept, lacking even the identity of a name, who tells of his Odyssey through a Negro college in the South, then to Harlem where he is hired by the Communists as their mass leader ("How would you like to be the new Booker T. Washington?") for $300 cash advance and the munificent, depression-period pay of $60 per week; he is quickly disillusioned and, battered in body and soul, finds refuge down a man-hole from whence to write a book about it all.

It would not be in order here to speak of responsibility, for the writer has anticipated and answered that objection in the prologue: "I can hear you say, 'What a horrible, irresponsible bastard!' And you're right. I leap to agree with you. I am one of the most irresponsible beings that ever lived."

Nor will I here attempt to refute the particular variations of the anti-Communist lie that Ellison tells. Some idea of his writing on this subject can be gained when we see even the *New Leader,* second to none in Red-baiting viciousness, complaining that "Ellison's Communists are hard to believe, they are so unrelievedly humorless, cynical and degenerate (including the black Communists)." And the *Nation's* reviewer—who says he is "ready to believe" the worst about "Harlem Stalinists"—grumbles: "The trouble with such caricature is that it undermines the intention behind it." (Nevertheless he finds the book "exalted.")

And just as the author makes his irresponsibility undebatable, so does he help establish the fact that his work is alien to the Negro people and has its source in upper-class corruption. According to an interview in the *Saturday Review* it was "T. S. Eliot's 'The Waste Land' which . . . changed the direction of his life: 'Eliot said something to my sensibilities that I couldn't find in Negro poets who wrote of experiences I myself had gone through.' "

Indeed, there is nothing in common between the wailing eunuchs of decay on the one hand, and the passionate strength and beauty of Negro poetry on the other. One can only speculate as to what it was in Ellison's "sensibilities" that drew him to Eliot and away from his people—and away from all people. But the result of the infection is a tragedy: the firstborn of a talented young Negro writer enters the world with no other life than its maggots.

Ellison is also a disciple of the Richard Wright–Chester Himes school and shares with these writers their bitter alienation from the Negro people, their hatred and contempt of the Negro working masses, their renegades' malice—and their servility to the masters. Cut off from the surging mainstream of Negro life and struggle and creativity, they stagnate in Paris, wander on lonely crusades, or spit out at the world from a hole in the ground.

But against them and their inspirers is the growing renaissance of the Negro people's culture—writers, playwrights, poets, singers, musicians, dancers, artists and actors, who are linked with their people, who *love* their people and who sing with the Negro poet of long ago:

> *"Lord, I don't want to be like Judas*
> *In my heart. . . ."*

Irving Howe: Black Boys and Native Sons

. . . What astonishes one most about *Invisible Man* is the apparent freedom it displays from the ideological and emotional penalties suffered by Negroes in this country—I say "apparent" because the freedom is not quite so complete as the book's admirers like to suppose. Still, for long stretches *Invisible Man* does escape the formulas of protest, local color, genre quaintness and jazz chatter. No white man could have written it, since no white man could know with such intimacy the life of the Negroes from the inside; yet Ellison writes with an ease and humor which are now and again simply miraculous.

Invisible Man is a record of a Negro's journey through contemporary America, from South to North, province to city, naïve faith to disenchantment and perhaps beyond. There are clear allegorical intentions (Ellison is "literary" to a fault) but with a book so rich in talk and drama it would be a shame to neglect the fascinating surface for the mere depths. The beginning is both nightmare and farce. A timid Negro boy comes to a white smoker in a Southern town: he is to be awarded a scholarship. Together with several other Negro boys he is rushed to the front of the ballroom, where a sumptuous blonde tantalizes and frightens them by dancing in the nude. Blindfolded, the Negro boys stage a "battle royal," a free-for-all in which they pummel each other to the drunken shouts of the whites. Practical jokes, humiliations, terror—and then the boy delivers a prepared speech of gratitude to his white benefactors. At the end of this section, the boy dreams that he has opened the briefcase given him together with his scholarship to a Negro college and that he finds an inscription reading: "To Whom It May Concern: Keep This Nigger-Boy Running."

He keeps running. He goes to his college and is expelled for having innocently taken a white donor through a Negro ginmill which also happens to be a brothel. His whole experience is to follow this pattern. Strip down a pretense, whether by choice or accident, and you will suffer penalties, since the rickety structure of Negro respectability rests upon pretense and those who profit from it cannot bear to have the reality exposed (in this case, that the college is dependent upon the Northern white millionaire). The boy then leaves for New York, where he works in a white-paint factory, becomes a soapboxer for the Harlem Communists, the darling of the fellow-travelling bohemia, and a big

From "*Black Boys and Native Sons*" in A World More Attractive, *by Irving Howe (New York: Horizon Press, 1963), pp. 98–122. Copyright © 1963 by Irving Howe. Reprinted by permission of the author and the publisher.*

The bulk of the original essay is devoted to Wright and Baldwin. Omissions are indicated by ellipses.

wheel in the Negro world. At the end, after witnessing a frenzied race riot in Harlem, he "finds himself" in some not entirely specified way, and his odyssey from submission to autonomy is complete.

Ellison has an abundance of that primary talent without which neither craft nor intelligence can save a novelist: he is richly, wildly inventive; his scenes rise and dip with tension, his people bleed, his language sings. No other writer has captured so much of the hidden gloom and surface gaiety of Negro life.

There is an abundance of superbly-rendered speech: a West Indian woman inciting her men to resist an eviction, a Southern sharecropper calmly describing how he seduced his daughter, a Harlem street-vender spinning jive. The rhythm of Ellison's prose is harsh and nervous, like a beat of harried alertness. The observation is expert: he knows exactly how zootsuiters walk, making stylization their principle of life, and exactly how the antagonism between American and West Indian Negroes works itself out in speech and humor. He can accept his people as they are, in their blindness and hope:—here, finally, the Negro world does exist, seemingly apart from plight or protest. And in the final scene Ellison has created an unforgettable image: "Ras the Destroyer," a Negro nationalist, appears on a horse dressed in the costume of an Abyssinian chieftain, carrying spear and shield, and charging wildly into the police—a black Quixote, mad, absurd, unbearably pathetic.

But even Ellison cannot help being caught up with *the idea* of the Negro. To write simply about "Negro experience," with the esthetic distance urged by the critics of the fifties, is a moral and psychological impossibility, for plight and protest are inseparable from that experience, and even if less political than Wright and less prophetic than Baldwin, Ellison knows this quite as well as they do.

If *Native Son* is marred by the ideological delusions of the thirties, *Invisible Man* is marred, less grossly, by those of the fifties. The middle section of Ellison's novel, dealing with the Harlem Communists, does not ring quite true, in the way a good portion of the writings on this theme during the post-war years does not ring quite true. Ellison makes his Stalinist figures so vicious and stupid that one cannot understand how they could ever have attracted him or any other Negro. That the party leadership manipulated members with deliberate cynicism is beyond doubt, but this cynicism was surely more complex and guarded than Ellison shows it to be. No party leader would ever tell a prominent Negro Communist, as one of them does in *Invisible Man:* "You were not hired [as a functionary] to think"—even if that were what he felt. Such passages are almost as damaging as the propagandist outbursts in *Native Son*.

Still more troublesome, both as it breaks the coherence of the novel and reveals Ellison's dependence on the post-war *Zeitgeist,* is the sudden, unprepared and implausible assertion of unconditioned freedom with which the novel ends. As the hero abandons the Communist Party he wonders, "Could politics ever be an expression of love?" This question, more portentous than profound, cannot easily be reconciled to a character who has been presented mainly as a passive victim of his experience. Nor is one easily persuaded by the hero's discovery that "my world has become one of infinite possibilities," his refusal to be the "invisible man" whose body is manipulated by various social groups. Though the unqualified assertion of self-liberation was a favorite strategy among American literary people in the fifties, it is also vapid and insubstantial. It violates the reality of social life, the interplay between external conditions and personal will, quite as much as the determinism of the thirties. The unfortunate fact remains that to define one's individuality is to stumble upon social barriers which stand in the way, all too much in the way, of "infinite possibilities." Freedom can be fought for, but it cannot always be willed or asserted into existence. And it seems hardly an accident that even as Ellison's hero asserts the "infinite possibilites" he makes no attempt to specify them. . . .

Anthony West: Black Man's Burden

Ralph Ellison's first novel, *Invisible Man* (Random House), is an exceptionally good book and in parts an extremely funny one. That is not to say that it is without defects, but since they are almost entirely confined to the intolerably arty prologue and epilogue, and to certain expressionist passages conveniently printed in italics, they can easily be skipped, and they should be, for they are trifling in comparison with its virtues. What gives it its strength is that it is about being colored in a white society and yet manages not to be a grievance book; it has not got the whine of a hard-luck story about it, and it has not got the blurting, incoherent quality of a statement made in anger. What gives it its character is a robust courage; it walks squarely up to color the way seventeenth-century writing walks up to mortality and death, to look it in the face as a part of the human situation that has to be lived with. Mr. Ellison's hero is a Negro of the South who starts out with the naïve illusion that what stands between him and the whites is a matter of education. He is given a scholarship to a Southern college that has been endowed by Northern philanthropists, and he goes to it in great delight, thinking that what he will learn there will

"Black Man's Burden" by Anthony West. From The New Yorker, *XXVIII (May 31, 1952), 79–81. Copyright © 1952 by The New Yorker Magazine, Inc. Reprinted by permission of the author and the publisher.*

pare away all his disabilities and disadvantages. He finds that the college cannot do that for him and does not even try to do it; it is concerned only with helping him make realistic adjustments to things as they are. He gets into a mess of trouble and is expelled. Before expelling him, the dean tells him just what the facts of colored life are:

> "You have some vague notions about dignity. . . . You have some white folk backing you and you don't want to face them because nothing is worse for a black man than to be humiliated by white folk. I know all about that too. . . . But you'll get over it; it's foolish and expensive and a lot of dead weight. You let the white folk worry about pride and dignity—you learn where you are and get yourself power, influence, contacts with powerful and influential people—then stay in the dark and use it!"

He is too young and too nobly stubborn to believe that this is the best that can be done with his life, and the rest of the book deals with his attempts to force the world to accept him on a pride-and-dignity basis, and with his final realization that he has to stay in the dark as an invisible man. This could easily be a glum and painful performance, but Mr. Ellison has the real satirical gift for handling ideas at the level of low comedy, and when he is most serious he is most funny. The technique is that of which *Candide* is the supreme example, but there is nothing archaic about the writing, which has an entirely contemporary vitality and a quite unexpected depth.

The first chapter is a little slow, but the second and third, which describe the trouble that leads to the hero's expulsion, convince one that Mr. Ellison is a writer with much more than promise. The hero is asked by the dean to drive one of the white Northern patrons of the college on a brief afternoon airing. By an unlucky chance, he takes the man past the house of the most notorious Negro no-good in the neighborhood, a man who is the embodiment of what Negro progressives call, and with hatred, field niggerism. The Northerner insists on stopping and talking to the monster, and a scene ensues that is an extraordinary piece of comic invention. Even when it is read over in a cold, analytical frame of mind and its purely entertaining aspects are set aside, it stands out as a startlingly good piece of writing. The monster's account of his misdeeds is in itself a tour de force—at once a brilliant parody of a kind of Southern genre writing about Negroes and an acute description of a psychopath's feeling about his actions, which includes, in a couple of sentences, a deadly cartoon of the relations between a genuine psychopathic criminal and members of the more optimistic schools of psychiatry. But excellent as that is, it is nothing to what Mr. Ellison makes the passage do on a more serious level. The student's reaction to the monster's story takes one deep into the feeling of one sort of Negro about another, but his reaction to the Northerner's reception of it takes one even further—into the heart of the very complex feeling between races. The Northerner's philanthropic interest in Negro education is a cover for a form of prurience, a voyeur's fascination. His real interest is in the Negro as an inferior kind of man, closer to the animal, more capable of letting drive on the lines of instinctive impulse and less restrained by civilized morality and patterns of conduct. Giving money to the college offers him a high-toned way of getting as close to these dark possibilities as he dares. It is easy to accuse Mr. Ellison of letting racial paranoia get out of hand in this particular character, and of producing an overdrawn caricature in consequence. But the attitude he is describing is a fairly common one, and is often given direct expression—even by writers of great delicacy and sensibility—despite its offensiveness. A poem called "The African," in the Literary Supplement of the London *Times* a while ago, put it very flatly:

> . . . I fell to brooding
> On bronze-dark features facing me, the glazed
> Soft shine of jet-black eyes; on what a London
> His Congo-born, his secret vision gazed
> So gently, mournfully; beyond his waking
> Quiet behavior what still potent background
> Vast and primeval worked, what violence
> Ancestral under silences profound.

The poem, presumably toying with some symbolism about a gracious innocence, went on to compare the man to swans on a pond, but even so it is hard to think that it would be pleasant to be on the receiving end of this sort of thing. Mr. Ellison tries to show just what it is like to take it from behind bronze-dark features, and does so remarkably well.

A good deal of the book is concerned with penetrating to the unease and self-consciousness that underlie a great many earnest white progressive approaches to The Question. After the student is kicked out of college, he goes North to try to make his way in New York, and his adventures are told in a highly imaginative, picaresque story, but, though the storytelling is excellent, in the end the impressive thing is the analysis of attitudes that rises out of each situation; there are always such sharpness of observation, such awareness of shades of feeling, at work. The hero is caught up in what is clearly an agitprop apparatus of the Communist Party (Mr. Ellison does not, though, give it that name) that is exploiting the color situation in Harlem. He is a natural speaker and he is made use of in campaigns as a front for the white committee. There is not only perceptive writing about the feeling between Negro and white in this part of the book but there is also perhaps the best description of rank-and-file Communist Party activity that has yet appeared in an American novel. The endless com-

mittee discussions of tactics, and the postmortems after the hero's
speeches, in which the nature and extent of his departures from "cor-
rect" lines are thrashed out, have an absolute authenticity. So has the
picture of the way in which the interplay of personalities inside the
movement, and the constant intriguing to use the Party disciplinary
machinery to advance one clique and set back another, takes place.
At last, the hero discerns the rank stink of falsity in the Party line
about color, partly through catching on to the way in which a white
Comrade who has married a colored girl makes play with the fact to
strengthen his hand in policy discussions of district tactics, partly
through a realization that the white Comrades have used him as a
lure, and a Negro gull to gull other Negroes. He sees that his district
leader, Brother Jack, is just as much Marse Jack as a field boss in a
white-supremacy state. The description of his disillusion with the
Party, a true agon, which is also his final understanding that there is
no external machine that can produce any ready-made solution either
to the color problem or to his own perplexities, is as moving and vivid
a piece of writing on this difficult subject as one could wish to read.

The book ends with a second tour de force, as successful as the
brilliant comedy scene in the Southern college town that is, in effect,
the book's starting point. The Party has lost control of its agitation
campaign as a result of what at first seems to the hero to be a typical
tactical blunder, and the mass support that it has won drifts over to a
straight anti-Communist and anti-white agitator called Ras, whose
wild speeches bring on a wave of rioting and looting. The drift into
disorder and the spread of violence are astonishingly well described in
realistic terms, and through it all Mr. Ellison never loses touch with
his gift for comic invention. As the riot builds up, the hero realizes
that not only have the Communists an unfriendly interest in him but
that he is due for unpleasantness from Ras's strong-arm men, who have
him marked down as their enemy and a tool of the whites. He disguises
himself in bourgeois finery, but the colored glasses and white hat he
dons to put him across the class frontier also turn him into the double
of a numbers racketeer called Rinehart, who is heavily involved in
quite enough trouble for two men. The hero's evasions as all Harlem
comes apart have a real nightmare humor. And in the middle of it
all, as the riot squads and the mounted police move in and shooting
begins, he suddenly sees what is happening. The Party has not made a
tactical blunder at all; it has deliberately surrendered its mass following to Ras in order to provoke violence, so that colored martyrs shot
down by the police, can be exploited in the next phase of agitation in
the district. The hero emerges in his own identity to warn the inno-
cents he has helped to fool what is being done to them. But Mr.
Ellison has a tight grip on his satiric comedy, and he is not going to
let his buffoon hero escape into tragedy; martyrdom is not to be *his*

fate. A gang of white looters chase him up a dark street, and he falls through an open manhole into a coal cellar. The whites, enraged by this surprising vanishing trick, slam the manhole cover down and leave him lying there helpless while the riot burns itself out above.

Few writers can have made a more commanding first appearance. Up to a point, *Invisible Man* resembles Céline's "Death on the Installment Plan." Its humor recalls the jokes that hang on Céline's fraudulent scientist, with his ascents in worn-out and patched balloons, his absurd magazine, and his system of electromagnetic plant culture, but Ellison's jokes are on the whole funnier, and his satire is much more convincing because there is clearly visible behind it—as there is not in Céline—a positive alternative to the evils he is attacking, the knowledge of a better way without which all satire becomes merely an empty scolding. It is a pity that Mr. Ellison's direct statement of the better way takes the form it does in the prologue and the epilogue, since they are the two worst pieces of writing. But the ideas toward which they fumble are as dignified as they are impressive, and it is perhaps unnecessary to have this direct statement, as they are so plainly implied in the rest of the book. It is not merely the Negro who has to realize that the only escape from the rattrap of worry about what one is or is not is to abandon the constant tease of self-consciousness. The Invisible Man of Mr. Ellison's title is the unattached man of Aldous Huxley's Perennial Philosophy, the man with courage to be utterly indifferent to himself and to his place in the world, the man who is alone free to be fully a man.

Richard D. Lehan: The Strange Silence of Ralph Ellison

The circumstances surrounding the publication and reception of Ralph Ellison's *Invisible Man* are, in many ways, strange. Strange, first, because in this novel Ellison revealed an obvious talent, winning the National Book Award when it was published in 1953,[1] and then remaining silent for twelve years, publishing only some essays but not another novel. Strange, secondly, because this novel, which has a number of serious artistic faults, kept the literary spotlight for those twelve years while Negro novels—like Richard Wright's *Native Son*

"The Strange Silence of Ralph Ellison" by Richard D. Lehan. From California English Journal, I, no. 2 (1965), 63–68. Copyright © 1965 by California English Journal. Reprinted by permission of the author and California English Journal.

Omitted here is the author's discussion of the probable nature of the new novel with which it seemed, in 1965, Ellison was about to break his "strange silence."

[1] [This is an error; *Invisible Man* was published in 1952 and Ellison won the National Book Award in 1953—Ed.]

and *The Outsider,* Baldwin's *Go Tell It on the Mountain* and *Giovanni's Room*—had their day and were soon forgotten, and other Negro novels—like Warren Miller's *The Cool World*—did not even have their day.[2]

Perhaps the most serious fault in *Invisible Man* is the obtrusive symbolism. The novel is a journey into self, or (to use the cliché) a search for identity, the unnamed Negro protagonist trying to discover the well-spring of his nature and come by some sense of ego in an alien world.

The terminology here is, of course, Freud's, and this is what is so obvious. Ellison structures the novel so that his hero comes by various forms of the superego (that is, the restraining voice of society) which arrest the id (that is, his libidinal energy) in his quest for self (ego).

There are many forms of the superego in the novel. Some of them are superbly handled. For example, the novel opens at a kind of civic stag party, where the protagonist and his Negro friends are blindfolded and set to boxing each other, and then to fighting for small change on a rug wired with electric current, all for the enjoyment of the town leaders, who fill the young hero with terror.

Even more effective are the scenes with the hero at college, the college being another version of the superego. There the president (Dr. Bledsoe) is really the puppet of Mr. Norton who is white, wealthy, powerful, and the college's benefactor. Mr. Norton thinks of the Negro as an abstract extension (the word *abstract* is important) of his personal destiny. Dr. Bledsoe endeavours to preserve this God-subject relationship between Norton and the Negro. By keeping Norton in contact with only the most idealistic aspects of Negro existence, Bledsoe is able to keep him in contact with a nonentity, an abstraction, an invisible man. Norton is a symbolic Godhead, the college a symbolic Garden of Paradise. The symbols, as you can see, are becoming more obvious, perhaps even reducing the complexity of what Ellison is saying, especially when the protagonist sees a snake cross the highway when he is expelled from this Eden for accidentally exposing Mr. Norton to the realities of Negro life. Yet Ellison is still in control here, and the college scenes have a haunting poignancy. Nameless and without precise location, the college has an air of other-worldliness. Norton visits the school each spring; his presence accompanies the cycles of life, and the campus is beautifully in bloom; but beneath the appearance of life and fecundity is the stark reality of arid death.

[2] [This list requires comment. Wright's work continues to be highly regarded by all serious readers of Afro-American fiction, and *Native Son* (1940) sells well enough three decades after publication to be thought of as a classic black novel. Baldwin's reputation is perhaps more dubious. And of course Warren Miller was a white author—ED.]

"Why is it," the hero asks, "that I can recall no fountain but one that was broken, corroded and dry?" [3]

If the scenes at the college are controlled, the scenes at the Golden Day are not. The Golden Day is a hang-out for the shell-shocked veterans who are housed near by. The hero takes Mr. Norton there when Mr. Norton passes out after his discussion with Jim Trueblood, who describes, in terms too graphic for Norton, the night he committed incest with his daughter. The veterans are an unruly lot; they cavort about in a mad and frenetic way—or perhaps I should say in a mad and libidinal way. "I'm a dynamo of energy. I come [here] to charge my batteries," one of the vets says. The vets are restrained by "an attendant, a kind of censor." The censor's name is not Superego; that would perhaps be too obvious; but it is the next obvious thing—his name is Supercargo:

> "WHAT'S GOING ON DOWN THERE?" a voice shouted from the balcony. Everyone turned. I saw a huge black giant of a man, dressed only in white shorts, swaying on the stairs. It was Supercargo, the attendant. I hardly recognized him without his hard-starched white uniform. Usually he walked around threatening the men with a strait jacket which he always carried over his arm, and usually they were quiet and submissive in his presence. But now they seemed not to recognize him and began shouting curses. (p. 76)

When the vets overcome Supercargo, they literally go wild, whirling about like maniacs. The boy tries to get Mr. Norton away, but he is cut off by the calmest of the vets, a man of shrewd disposition who tells Norton, to the boy's growing consternation, that

> "The clocks are all set back and the forces of destruction are rampant down below. They might suddenly realize that you are what you are, and then your life wouldn't be worth a piece of bankrupt stock. You would be canceled, perforated, voided, become the recognized magnet attracting loose screws. Then what would you do? Such men are beyond money, and with Supercargo down, out like a felled ox, they know nothing of value. To some, you are the great white father, to others the lyncher of souls, but for all, you are confusion come even into the Golden Day." (pp. 85–86)

Scenes like this, obvious in their meaning, mechanical and labored in their method, impair the purity of the novel's design. What Ellison has to say is very important; some symbols come up to the complexity of his thought (the broken fountain in the college, the dynamo that pulses in the night in a kind of libidinal way and which the boy hears when there is a pause in Mr. Barbee's, the founder's, arid speech); but

---

[3] Ralph Ellison, *Invisible Man* (New York, 1960), p. 38. All further references are from the paperback edition which is more readily available than the Random House edition (New York, 1952).

many symbols (and the Golden Day is one) are contrived and forced, creating a world of their own which wrenches us from scene to scene, where the pastoral world gives way suddenly and unexpectedly to the grotesque, and where things seem to happen just beyond our myopic sight, and people scream to us in silent voices.

Symbolism in *Invisible Man* becomes, that is, too much of a device, a way of communicating the problem without having to experience or feel it. Take the symbolism of blindness: Homer A. Barbee, who extols the work of Bledsoe, is blind. Jack, the Communist who sees the Negro in terms of a group caught in a dialectical process, has a glass eye. The hero himself is initially blinded by his ambitions; at the town meeting he is appropriately blindfolded. Even the briefcase the hero carries is a repository of symbolic objects the narrator picks up on his journey— a toy bank in the image of a Negro, a Negro puppet manipulated by an invisible black string, a link in a leg chain—all of which depict the Negro, in an obvious and mechanical way, as an economic pawn.

It is thus odd that a novel this mechanical can have received such continued attention and praise. The answer rests in the fact that *Invisible Man* is strange in a third way—a way that is perhaps its salvation and which explains why it has lived these twelve years. For *Invisible Man* is a novel about a Negro but is not really a Negro novel. The unnamed hero happens to be a Negro, and his story has relevance because he is a Negro, but there is a larger dimension to this novel, which Irving Howe in his recent exchange with Ellison has not been able to see. Ellison's hero attempts to create the consciousness of his race by creating his own consciousness, and unlike (say) Richard Wright's *Native Son, Invisible Man* is no more a Negro protest novel than is James Joyce's *A Portrait of the Artist as a Young Man*. Ellison's novel depicts, in a truly brilliant way, the feeling that beneath layer upon layer of life—life superimposed upon the Negro who has been cut off from his native culture—is an uncontaminated well-spring, an uninhibited realm where impulse and passion can be released like a dark breeze. Ellison's interest in jazz is in part an interest in the means one can use to find the path back to such a source.

The hero in *Invisible Man* is also looking for such a path, first unknowingly and finally with a heightened sense of conscious awareness. In fact, he develops a sense of self-irony, and he moves from seeing himself seriously to seeing himself comically, acting the expected part while secretly laughing at the white man. But before he can find out who he is, he has to find out who he is not. The logic of the novel is to show him moving through various forms of life—really various forms of death—rejecting each form as he comes to understand in what way it can destroy him. The narrator, for example, rejects Jack and the Brotherhood because he realizes that to Jack he is only an economic pawn to be thought of in terms of a dialectical process of history. He rejects Ras the Exhorter, a black nationalist, whose belief in Negro racial supremacy fires Ras to violence. He rejects Mary, the prototypal mother, who wants him to be careful, to conform, to succeed in the white man's world. He rejects Lucius Brockway, a Negro who wants to see other Negroes kept in their place so they will be no threat to him. These experiences—with the Communist Party, the race supremists, the possessive mother, the jealous colleague—go beyond Negro reality to explore something common to both white and black in twentieth century life.

These experiences involve, however, complete rejection; invisible man rejects all these forms of anti-life; and he is left in the end without anything more to reject—and without anything to affirm; he ends alone, abandoned, on an underground coal pile. The coal pile becomes a retreat from society, a place of isolation and of silence—for Ellison a twelve-year silence. There is a double symbolism here—one political and social, the other literary and aesthetic. *Invisible Man* is a journey for Ellison himself as well as for his hero, and he makes this clear in *Shadow and Act,* a recently published collection of essays. The symbolic journey parallels the act of literary creation, the author, here Ellison, experiencing various forms of life vicariously, testing them in his imagination, and so discovering himself through technique, through the crucible of literary form. Just as the romantic poets believed they came to a heightened sense of life through contact with nature, Ellison sees the process of writing as a kind of flaming vortex that tempers and purifies the soul.

The end of the novel is the beginning for both Ellison and his hero —it brings his hero to an awareness of who he is not, and this is the real starting point in his life, although it is the point at which the novel ends:

> And now I realized [concludes the narrator] that I couldn't return to Mary's, or to any part of my old life. I could approach it only from the outside, and I had been as invisible to Mary as I had been to the Brotherhood. No, I couldn't return to Mary's or to the campus, or to the Brotherhood, or home. I could only move ahead or stay here, underground. So I would stay here until I was chased out. Here, at least, I could try to think things out in peace, or, if not in peace, in quiet. I would take up residence underground. The end was in the beginning. (p. 494)

Ellison could not take his main character beyond history, and in 1952 there was nothing else to which his hero could commit himself, and he stays underground where there is at least peace and quiet. . . .

Ernest Kaiser: Negro Images in American Writing

. . . To Ellison, Negro life in America is merely a part of the general human condition of Western man to be mastered individually by each Negro as a man. He doesn't like the sociological description of the Negroes' struggles and suffering in the ghetto, for he thinks that the sociological account reduces the Negro and denies his humanity and cultural heritage. But he is mistaken here; the two go together. They are not mutually exclusive at all. Following André Malraux, the existentialists, the disillusioned or clever, opportunistic attackers of the left and the New Critics who emphasize form as supreme, even determining content, Ellison has become an Establishment writer, an Uncle Tom, an attacker of the sociological formulations of the civil rights movement, a defender of the criminal Vietnam war of extermination against the Asian (and American Negro) people, a denigrator of the great tradition of Negro protest writing and, worst of all for himself as a creative artist, a writer of weak and ineffectual fiction and essays mostly about himself and how he became an artist. (See the chapter from his forthcoming novel "It Always Breaks Out" [*Partisan Review*, Spring 1963], several pieces in *Shadow and Act* [1964], "Tell It Like It Is, Baby" [*The Nation*, September 20, 1965] and the interviews of him—"An American Novelist Who Sometimes Teaches" [*N. Y. Times Magazine*, Nov. 20, 1966] and "A Very Stern Discipline" [*Harper's*, March 1967].) And ironically enough, Ellison has developed in this way and reached these conclusions at the very time when the Negro people's liberation struggle has reached new heights; when writers like John O. Killens, the late Lorraine Hansberry, Langston Hughes, Ronald L. Fair, Margaret Walker, William Melvin Kelley, James Baldwin, Paule Marshall, Ossie Davis, Loften Mitchell, Lerone Bennett, Jr., John Henrik Clarke and other Negro writers have delineated in novels, short stories, plays and trenchant essays the Negro people's aspirations and heroic struggles.

From "Negro Images in American Writing" by Ernest Kaiser in Freedomways, VII (Spring 1967), 152–63. Copyright © 1967 by Freedomways Associates, Inc. Reprinted by permission of Freedomways Magazine.

The original essay is a review of Images of the Negro in American Literature, eds. Seymour L. Gross and John Edward Hardy (Chicago: University of Chicago Press, 1966). The bulk of the review is omitted here.

Chronology of Important Dates

	Ellison	The Age
1910		Approximately 75 percent of black Americans reported in census as rural; W. E. B. Du-Bois begins editing *The Crisis* for the newly incorporated NAACP; Urban League organized.
1914	Born March 1 of parents who had migrated from South Carolina to Oklahoma	Joyce's *Portrait of the Artist as a Young Man* published.
1915		Booker T. Washington dies; the Great Migration to northern cities begins.
1919		Twenty-five race riots take place during the "Red Summer."
1920	Attends Frederick Douglass School in Oklahoma City.	Two-thirds of Manhattan's black population resides in Harlem, the setting for the First International Convention of (Marcus Garvey's) United Negro Improvement Association attended by 25,000 delegates.
1922		T. S. Eliot's *The Waste Land.* Joyce's *Ulysses.*
1925		Alain Locke's anthology of the Harlem Renaissance, *The New Negro;* Countee Cullen's *Color;* Langston Hughes's "The Negro Speaks of Rivers"; Garvey con-

		fined to the Atlanta Penitentiary.
1926		Hemingway's *The Sun Also Rises*.
1928		Sixth World Congress of International Communist Party adopts policy of advocating self-determination for Negroes in the United States; Claude McKay's *Home to Harlem*.
1929	Hears Lester Young playing with members of the Blue Devils Orchestra—predecessor of Basie's band.	William Faulkner's *Sartoris* and *The Sound and the Fury*.
1930		Black Muslim movement founded in Detroit; Langston Hughes's *Not Without Laughter*.
1933	Goes to Tuskegee Institute to study music.	Government sponsorship of arts begins under PWA and WPA.
1935		Hemingway's *Green Hills of Africa*.
1936	Goes to New York City with the intention of studying sculpture with Richmond Barthé. Here he meets Richard Wright.	Count Basie's band, including Jimmy Rushing and Lester Young, comes to New York from the Middle West. Alain Locke's *Negro Art Past and Present*.
1937	Publishes first work—a review —in *New Challenge*, edited by Wright; goes to Dayton with brother.	
1938	With Federal Writers' Project.	
1939–41	Contributing fiction, sketches, and reports to *New Masses*.	
1940		Richard Wright's *Native Son*.
1942	Editor of *Negro Quarterly*.	Communist party of the United States opposes A. Philip Randolph's plan for a protest march on Washington; Dizzy Gillespie, Thelonius Monk, Charlie Christian, Charlie Parker, and other musicians gather-

		ing at Minton's Playhouse, mark the beginning of bop and cool jazz. Atlanta University begins "Annual Exhibition of Work by Negro Artists."
1943		Race riots in Detroit and Harlem.
1943–45	Serves in Merchant Marine.	
1945	Rosenwald Grant; begins writing *Invisible Man*.	End of World War II.
1946	Marries Fanny McConnell.	
1947–48	Battle Royal section of *Invisible Man* published in English and American magazines.	
1950		NAACP attorneys win several cases that begin to undermine segregation.
1952	*Invisible Man* published.	
1953	National Book Award; Russwurm Award.	James Baldwin's *Go Tell It on the Mountain*.
1954	Participant in Salzburg Seminar.	Supreme Court decision outlaws school segregation. Hemingway wins Nobel Prize for Literature.
1955		Montgomery bus boycott led by Martin Luther King; Charlie Parker dies.
1958–61	Instructor in Russian and American Literature at Bard College.	
1960		Census reports 73 percent of "nonwhite" population lives in the cities, 48 percent of the total in the North and West; Sit-ins begin February in Greensboro, North Carolina.
1963		March on Washington for jobs and freedom.
1964	*Shadow and Act;* teaching creative writing at Rutgers; Fellow in American Studies at Yale.	*Autobiography of Malcolm X;* LeRoi Jones's *Dutchman* and *The Slave* produced.

1965   *Book Week* poll chooses *Invis-*   Malcolm X assassinated.
            ible Man as the most distin-
            guished novel of the previous
            twenty years.

1966   Black Panther party founded.

1967   Organization of Black Ameri-
                                                     can Culture (OBAC) begins
                                                     painting Wall of Respect in
                                                     Chicago.

1968   Martin Luther King assassi-
                                                     nated; Eldridge Cleaver's *Soul
                                                     on Ice.*

Notes on the Editor and Contributors

JOHN M. REILLY, editor of this volume, is Associate Professor of English at the State University of New York at Albany. He earned his Ph.D at Washington University (St. Louis) with a dissertation on Richard Wright and has published articles on Jean Toomer and James Baldwin. Currently he is working as a coeditor on an anthology of Afro-American literature.

LLOYD L. BROWN has been managing editor of *New Masses* and an associate editor of *Masses & Mainstream*. Besides reviews and critical essays, he has published short stories and a novel, *Iron City*.

ROBERT BONE, Professor of Literature at Teachers College, Columbia University, is best known for his critical-historical study *The Negro Novel in America*. Since its publication he has also written specialized studies of James Baldwin and William Demby.

SELMA FRAIBERG is a member of the staff of Children's Psychiatric Hospital in Ann Arbor, Michigan. Her professional publications include articles on psychoanalytic principles in casework and *The Magic Years: Understanding and Handling the Problems of Early Childhood*.

CHARLES I. GLICKSBERG, Professor of English at Brooklyn College of the City University of New York, writes extensively on modern literature. His books include *The Tragic Vision in Twentieth-Century Literature, The Ironic Vision in Modern Literature, Literature and Religion,* and *The Self in Modern Literature*.

ELLIN HOROWITZ, a graduate of Bennington College, has published critical articles in *Criticism* and other journals.

FLOYD R. HOROWITZ combines an understanding of computer technology with his knowledge of literature. He has written on Mark Twain's symbolic commentary as well as on the use of computers for research in the humanities. He serves as Associate Professor of English at the Univeristy of Kansas.

IRVING HOWE was a founder of *Dissent* and continues now as its editor. His varied interests are reflected in studies of the United Auto Workers and the Communist Party (USA), as well as criticism of Sherwood Anderson, William Faulkner, and other writers. *Steady Work* and *A World More Attractive* are collections of his critical essays. Currently he is Professor of English at Hunter College of the City University of New York.

ESTHER MERLE JACKSON has held Whitney, Fulbright, and Guggenheim grants. She received her Ph.D. from Ohio State University and has taught at Clark College and Shaw University. In addition, she has been associate editor of *Quarterly Journal of Speech* and is the author of *The Broken World of Tennessee Williams*.

ERNEST KAISER, a member of the staff of the Schomburg Library in New York City, is a contributing editor of *Freedomways* magazine, in which he has published among other pieces, a "Selected Bibliography of the Published Writings of W. E. B. DuBois," "The Literature of Harlem," and a bibliography on American Indians and Mexican Americans.

RICHARD D. LEHAN, Associate Professor of English at UCLA, is the author of *F. Scott Fitzgerald and the Craft of Fiction*. His critical articles include several studies of Existentialist themes in modern American fiction.

THERMAN B. O'DANIEL was a founder and now serves as editor of *CLA Journal*, the official publication of the College Language Association. He is also an administrator and teacher at Morgan State College, where he has been a staff member since 1956. Among his own recent contributions to the *CLA Journal* is a bibliography on Langston Hughes.

EARL H. ROVIT, Associate Professor of English at City College of the City University of New York, has been a Fulbright and Guggenheim Fellow. Among his publications on modern American authors are a comprehensive study of Ernest Hemingway and an essay on Saul Bellow's work.

WILLIAM J. SCHAFER is Assistant Professor of English at Berea College. In addition to the essay on irony and satire in *Invisible Man*, he has also written about the antihero in the novel.

M. K. SINGLETON earned a Ph.D. at Duke University and has taught American Literature at the University of Wisconsin and at San Diego State. He has also served as Walter Perry Johnson Scholar in Law at the University of California School of Jurisprudence.

ANTHONY WEST worked for the British Broadcasting Corporation from 1943 to 1945. He held the Houghton Mifflin Fellowship in 1947, and for many years has been a contributor to the *New Yorker*. Notable among his writings is a critical biography of D. H. Lawrence.

Selected Bibliography

Baumbach, Jonathan, "Nightmare of a Native Son: Ralph Ellison's *Invisible Man*," *Critique*, VI (1963), 48–65. This article finds the crucial flaw in the novel to be inconsistency of method, which shifts the narrative from surface realism to wild surrealism. From this observation the author concludes that the book is both static and susceptible to a heavily allegorical reading.

Christian, Barbara, "Ralph Ellison: A Critical Study," in *Black Expression*, ed. Addison Gayle, Jr. New York: Weybright and Talley, Inc., 1969, pp. 353–65. Noting that Ellison's critical writings and interviews are useful for showing his esthetic interests—thus helping to explain *Invisible Man*—the author points to the central significance of a concept of myth, and traces the narrator's progression from blindness to invisibility.

Hassan, Ihab Habib, *Radical Innocence, Studies in the Contemporary American Novel*. Princeton, N.J.: Princeton University Press, 1961. In a chapter on Buechner, Malamud, and Ellison, the author describes the ironic and tragi-comic character of the Invisible Man as a function of the ambiguity of the narrator's fate.

Horowitz, Floyd Ross, "The Enigma of Ellison's Intellectual Man," *CLA Journal*, VII (December 1963), 126–32. This essay posits an unresolved conflict between the characterization of the narrator as an intellectual and his inability to develop a moral philosophy.

Isaacs, Harold R., "Five Writers and Their African Ancestors," *Phylon*, XXI (Winter 1960), 317–22. Based on interviews with black authors, this discussion stresses Ellison's interest in a uniquely American experience and his disavowal of a significant relationship to Africa.

Killens, John O., "Invisible Man," *Freedom*, II (June 1952), 7. A leading black novelist's view of *Invisible Man*, this review takes strong exception to Ellison's representation of Afro-America, arguing that the novel dehumanizes black people.

Klein, Marcus, *After Alienation: American Novels in Mid-Century*. New York: The World Publishing Company, 1964. From the assumption that protest is a limiting motive Klein argues that *Invisible Man* is a success because of Ellison's rejection "not only of protest but of all social radicalism, of social consciousness itself, and of the notion of man as a static social fact."

Kostelanetz, Richard, "The Politics of Ellison's Booker: *Invisible Man* as Symbolic History," *Chicago Review,* XIX, no. 2 (1967), 5–26. This is a reading of the novel as an evaluation of the ideas of Booker T. Washington, the radical political movement, and black nationalism. The author concludes that Ellison's narrator rejects them all because they ruthlessly insist upon submission of the self to abstractions of reality.

Nash, Russell W., "Stereotypes and Social Types in Ellison's *Invisible Man,*" *The Sociological Quarterly,* VI (Autumn 1965), 349–60. Employing a conception developed by Orrin E. Klapp in *Heroes, Villains, and Fools* (Prentice-Hall, 1962) of a continuum running from negative stereotypes to authentic social types, this article argues the value of *Invisible Man* as a representation of changing social relationships, as well as a practical effort to encourage social morality.

Rodnon, Stewart, "Ralph Ellison's *Invisible Man:* Six Tentative Approaches," *CLA Journal,* XII (March 1969), 244–56. This article outlines familiar kinds of criticism but with explicit attention to their value in classroom teaching of the novel.

Stanford, Raney, "The Return of the Trickster: When a Not-a-Hero Is a Hero," *Journal of Popular Culture,* I (Winter 1967), 228–42. Using Rinehart and the narrator of *Invisible Man* as examples, this article describes the reappearance in modern literature of the primitive trickster. The primitive character coped with alien nature by his cunning; his modern counterpart uses roguery to cope with malevolent society.

Tischler, Nancy M. "Negro Literature and Classic Form," *Contemporary Literature,* X (Summer 1969), 352–65. This article, discussing Styron's *Confessions of Nat Turner* and Ellison's *Invisible Man* as examples respectively of modified classic tragedy and modified classic comedy in "Negro-centered" fiction exemplifies the problem in applying strictly formal criticism in the study of Afro-American literature.

TWENTIETH CENTURY

INTERPRETATIONS

MAYNARD MACK, *Series Editor*
Yale University

NOW AVAILABLE
Collections of Critical Essays
ON

(continued on next page)

(*continued from previous page*)

OEDIPUS REX
THE OLD MAN AND THE SEA
PAMELA
A PASSAGE TO INDIA
THE PLAYBOY OF THE WESTERN WORLD
THE PORTRAIT OF A LADY
A PORTRAIT OF THE ARTIST AS A YOUNG MAN
THE PRAISE OF FOLLY
PRIDE AND PREJUDICE
THE RAPE OF THE LOCK
THE RIME OF THE ANCIENT MARINER
ROBINSON CRUSOE
ROMEO AND JULIET
SAMSON AGONISTES
THE SCARLET LETTER
SIR GAWAIN AND THE GREEN KNIGHT
SONGS OF INNOCENCE AND OF EXPERIENCE
THE SOUND AND THE FURY
THE TEMPEST
TESS OF THE D'URBERVILLES
TOM JONES
TO THE LIGHTHOUSE
THE TURN OF THE SCREW
TWELFTH NIGHT
UTOPIA
VANITY FAIR
WALDEN
THE WASTE LAND
WOMEN IN LOVE
WUTHERING HEIGHTS